# Praise for *From*

"This book will unpack the nuts and bolts of matri... of your marriage."

—Dr. Kevin Leman, *New York Times* Bestselling Author of *Sheet Music* and *Have a New Husband by Friday*

"Lucille Williams writes about marriage with refreshing honesty and candor. You will find her direct approach in addressing the difficulties of marriage to be challenging, and you will find her positive tone to be encouraging. I may have a shelf full of marriage books, but Lucille's vulnerable transparency, biblical clarity, and practical counsel makes *From Me to We* a book I will recommend not only to engaged couples but to couples who have been married for years."

—Kyle Idleman, Teaching Pastor at Southeast Christian Church, and Author of *Not a Fan* and *The End of Me*

"Are you approaching the altar? If you're an engaged couple looking for a how-to guide that is both very helpful and very funny, this is the book for you! Although Lu doesn't shy away from the tough conversations, she handles them in a way that is engaging and personal—and wise. This is a great read for a great start to a great marriage."

Shaunti Feldhahn, Bestselling Author of *For Women Only* and *For Men Only*

"In an age where the meaning of marriage has been lost, we need a book like *From Me to We*. Thankfully, Lucille Williams reminds us that marriage is not a contract to be negotiated, but rather it is a covenant to be honored. I know you will find this book helpful as you think of what a marriage could and should look like!"

—Caleb Kaltenbach, Lead Pastor of Discovery Church and Author of *Messy Grace*

"Far too many engaged couples focus all their time and energy on the wedding day, when for the long-term benefit of their marriage relationship a good dose of premarital education could make the long-term difference of a loving relationship. I can't think of a better person in the world to help you get ready for your marriage than Lucille Williams. She is authentic, vulnerable, practical, and fun. I love the matter-of-fact, practical way she writes, and her advice is the best. Invest in the success of your marriage before it begins."

—Jim Burns, PhD, President of HomeWord and Author of *Getting Ready for Marriage* and *Creating an Intimate Marriage*

"I have known Mike and Lucille for a long time, and the words shared and expressed in this book should be taken to heart. Lucille unpacks the 'what you are getting into' when you get married as well as the 'why.' With an authentic and relevant voice, Lucille unpacks practical advice for couples getting ready to embark on a lifetime of commitment and connection. Every couple setting out on their marital journey must read this book."

—Craig Jutila, President of Empowered Living, Inc. and Author of *From Hectic to Healthy* and *Faith and the Modern Family*

"There have been scores of books written on marriage, but to me, very few speak so loudly as Lucille Williams' book, *From Me to We*. Lucille's willingness to share about her own marriage journey with her husband of more than thirty years, as well as their path from non-belief to new life in Christ, will guide and inspire any couple to drink deeply from God's blessing that is the union of marriage. God is so good, and so is *From Me to We*."
—Frank Sontag, Christian Radio Host of "The Frank Sontag Show," 99.5 KKLA-FM, and Author of *Light the Way Home*

"Everyone goes into marriage wanting to live happily ever after—but not everyone receives the actual tools for a successful marriage. A wise person will seek out advice from couples who have been happily married for a long time and will take godly counsel to heart. In her latest book, *From Me to We*, Lucille Williams is your personal premarital mentor! I have known and served with Lucille and her husband, Mike, for many years. There is no better person to give honest, no-holds-barred wisdom for a Christ-honoring and joyful marriage. Lucille covers every possible topic, from communication and sex to money and in-laws. Read this book and set your marriage up for a lifetime of love and laughter!"
—Dudley Rutherford, Senior Pastor of Shepherd Church in Los Angeles, CA, and Author of *Walls Fall Down*

"I grew up in a family where marriage seemed to be a breeze. No fighting, no quarrels, not even a disagreement between my mother and father. That upbringing left me thinking the woman who married me was going to be the luckiest bride ever, because of everything I knew about marriage. Well, that all changed on the second day of our honeymoon when my wife and I both found ourselves saying, 'What were we thinking?' In that instant we realized quickly how much we had to learn about marriage. In her latest book, *From Me to We*, Lucille Williams covers a wide range of topics that will help couples avoid a great deal of frustration and disappointment as they explore the journey to becoming one. From the first chapter you will fall in love with her humor, passion, and burden for every couple embarking on the journey of becoming one."
—Tim Winters, Executive Pastor of Shepherd Church

"I've been married to an amazing woman for almost 30 years. I love her more today than I did the day we were married. But truth be told, I wish *From Me to We* had been available when we were preparing for marriage. Lucille Williams has written a beautiful guide that I believe will help many understand what a Christ-honoring covenant marriage is supposed to look like. Convicting and straightforward, Lucille does what many writers refuse to do. She tells the truth. I love her honest and compelling approach, and I plan to make *From Me to We* required reading for every couple that asks me to marry them. I loved this book, and I know you'll love it, too."
—Drew Sherman, Lead Pastor of Compass Christian Church, Dallas/Fort Worth, Texas

"Thriving marriages require more than high hopes and big dreams—staying in love requires a plan. Successful marriages don't just happen. . .they require intentional, positive steps in the right direction. Lucille Williams provides straight talk mixed with easy-to-do actions and dishes it out with humor and practical wisdom. *From Me to We* will set you up with the tools you need to love each other for the long haul."
—Doug Fields, Executive Director of the HomeWord Center for Youth & Family and Author of 50+ books, including *Married People: Helping Churches Help Marriages*; *7 Ways To Be Her Hero: the one your wife has been waiting for*, and *Getting Ready for Marriage*

# from me to we

A Premarital Guide for the Bride- and Groom-to-Be

## Lucille Williams

**SHILOH RUN** PRESS

An Imprint of Barbour Publishing, Inc.

Print ISBN 978-1-63409-863-2

eBook Editions:
Adobe Digital Edition (.epub) 978-1-68322-310-8
Kindle and MobiPocket Edition (.prc) 978-1-68322-311-5

Published in association with the literary agency of Credo Communications, LLC, Grand Rapids, Michigan, www.credocommunications.net.

Cover Design: Brand Navigation

Published by Shiloh Run Press, an imprint of Barbour Publishing, Inc., P.O. Box 719, Uhrichsville, Ohio 44683, www.shilohrunpress.com

*Our mission is to publish and distribute inspirational products offering exceptional value and biblical encouragement to the masses.*

Member of the
Evangelical Christian
Publishers Association

Printed in the United States of America.

# Contents

Me, me, me, me, me! We live in a culture consumed with self. No one is faulting you; it's the world we live in today. But your world is about to change, becoming more vibrant and beautiful, where two become one. Are you ready to create your fairy tale, your true-life blockbuster adventure film? One ingredient is critically essential: you must swap your "me" thinking for "we" thinking. Are you ready? . . .

My goal with this book is to guide you on your way with the start of a happy, healthy marriage. So put on your swim cap, 'cause we're divin' in!

# Chapter One
## Why Do People Keep Telling Us Marriage Is Hard?

People will tell you marriage is hard. Why? *Because it is!* But you get to decide how content you will be.

I will tell you marriage is not for the faint of heart. If you're ready to be hurt beyond anything you've ever experienced, then you may be ready. Just maybe. If you're ready to have your prayer life ignited, you may be ready. If you're ready to pack everything up—all of your friends, all of your family, all of your dreams—and repack with someone else, throwing your dirty laundry and theirs in one big heap, you may be ready.

Ready or not, many jump into "marital paradise." And then many jump back out again. How many people do you know who are divorced? How many of those weddings did you attend? Did you see it coming? Probably not. They probably didn't either. For many, marriage is not a paradise at all.

But for the fortunate among us, marriage creates a personal two-person paradise. Do you think this happens randomly? It does not. And you can have it, too. That *could* be you. Many men and women are extremely happy in their marriage. It *can* happen for you, too. Look around. Do you see any happily married couples? What makes them stand out among the rest?

## Too Young and Stupid to Get Married

I got engaged at eighteen. Yes, I was very young. And my prince? He seemed old to me at the time. Mike was twenty. A year later we said "I do." (Actually, we said "I will." The minister who performed our wedding told us to repeat "I will," and if I hadn't been overcome with emotion I might have screamed, "No, no, no! I want to say 'I do,' It's 'I do,' not 'I will!'" I have always felt cheated I didn't get to say "I do," since I had dreamed of doing so since I was a little girl.) Two weeks after my nineteenth birthday, I was a married woman. We had all the answers and cruised away into marital bliss.

And if you believed my last sentence, then you've watched too many chick flicks.

Let's get real! The only cruising we did in the beginning years of our marriage was on our honeymoon when we took an *actual* cruise.

Yes, we were young, which made the wedding and honeymoon all the more exhilarating and adventurous. I can recall thinking my life was like a fairy tale after the wedding was over. Everything was in place.

Sure, our wedding day had quite a few bumps—from my dad's tux not fitting to my future mother-in-law yelling at me while I was putting on my wedding dress.

Oh, and then there was the "little" fight Mike and I had the morning of our wedding when we vowed *not to get married.*

He was with his family, I was with mine, and we decided to talk on the phone. There was yelling and stress with my family and friction with his, and the anxious bride and groom decided we needed to talk. Instead of whispering sweet nothings to each other over the phone, we got into a fight, which escalated to screaming. And yes, there was a lot of name calling, too. And maybe some swearing. Yeah, not my finest hour. But you should know we weren't Christians then.

"He's a *JERK!*" I screamed to my brother-in-law. "I'm not going to marry him! Did you hear what he called me?" I can't remember exactly what my soon-to-be brother-in-law said, but somehow he got us talking again.

And the wedding was back on.

Our road to marital delight was a rocky one, for sure. We dated, got engaged, and married all without the help of knowing Jesus as Savior. It would have made the whole process immeasurably better had we been Christians, but we weren't. We were two young kids trying to figure it all out.

After over thirty-four years and raising three kids together, we are going stronger than ever. And did I mention my husband is a pastor? Yes, the young lady with the potty mouth became a pastor's wife. Miracles happen.

## Why Get Married Anyway?

First, I want to address the question: Why are you getting married? Stop and think for a minute.

Are you envisioning long walks on the beach, pancake breakfasts, chatting while making dinner together, and long nights of unbridled passion? If so, yes, you are normal. How do I know this? Because God made us for connectedness, and He created marriage—never forget that. The Bible states,

"Then the Lord God, said, 'It is not good for the man to be alone; I will make him a helper suitable for him'" (Genesis 2:18). God created the marriage union. "For this reason a man shall leave his father and his mother, and be joined to his wife; and they shall become one flesh. And the man and his wife were both naked and were not ashamed" (Genesis 2:24–25).

The covenant you are about to enter is a holy union. Holy and designed by God. You are making a vow for life. Not just until you don't feel like being married anymore. A promise *for life*. Take a look at 1 Corinthians 7:39: "A wife is bound as long as her husband lives; but if her husband is dead, she is free to be married to whom she wishes, only in the Lord." As long as your spouse is alive, you're bound to him or her. Are you ready to make such a heavy commitment? Yes, there could be circumstances out of your control, which could break your covenant with God and your spouse, such as abuse, abandonment, and/or adultery, but saying yes to marriage is entering into a holy contract. One God never intended to be broken. Have you thought about that?

Most likely, you're eager to get this "party" started. Stay with me. Answering the *why* is important. A healthy marriage begins *before* the wedding day. The better your start out of the marriage gate, the more harmony you will have and the better your marriage (and sex life!) will be.

During my honeymoon, I felt like I was living a fairy tale. We had decided on a Caribbean cruise. Everything was simply perfect. The beautiful ocean with bright sunny days and romantic nights. Food was endless and elegant, the ports were adventurous—we were enjoying our Caribbean paradise, and each other, more and more each day. If this was what marriage was like, I was all in! We overflowed with food and fun, eating like we were royalty. To be honest, *stuffed* would be more accurate; we *stuffed* ourselves with delectable food and fun.

Then the last night of our cruise jolted me back to reality. The day before the cruise ended and the ship docked, we had handed over most of our luggage. We packed everything except the clothes we were wearing and turned over our bags to the ship's crew. That night we ate to excess, as usual. We were seated at a big oval-shaped booth and were eating, laughing, and enjoying the company of three other couples. Mike and I were in the center, unable to get out from either side.

We were having an extremely good time until. . .*it happened*. Suddenly, my husband put his head back and began to vomit. As in barf, puke, heave, hurl! It was spewing out like a volcano, all over him and me!

Fairy tale over.

Silence. Everyone at the table sat in stunned silence. We excused ourselves and went to our tiny cabin room. But now we had a huge dilemma. The clothes we had on, now covered in vomit, were the only clothes we had. Everything else had been packed and taken away.

This is the part of the story where my resourceful wifey skills enter the scene. When one is covered in vomit and has a sick husband, one has to think fast. Turning into a female MacGyver, I was able to get some laundry detergent from one of the workers on the ship, and I washed our clothes in the tiny sink. In the tiny bathroom. In our tiny cabin room.

Being MacGyver wasn't adventurous at all.

As I washed the clothes in the sink, I recall looking down at the dirty, barf-covered clothes, and thinking, *This is marriage.* As young and naive as I was, I was right about that realization. Sometimes marriage is washing vomit out of clothes. Sometimes it's staying when everything inside of you wants to leave. Sometimes it's scrubbing all the stains out until you can't see them anymore. Sometimes it's patching up your broken heart. . .again.

If you want a strong marriage—one that honors God—you not only wrestle your own messes; you wrestle with your spouse's messes, too. You pull double duty! "This is marriage." He hurled. I cleaned it up. It "landed" on both of us.

But listen to the magic moment. *Don't miss this!* When you put your spouse before yourself, times when you're cleaning up barf are worth every ounce of angst in exchange for the countless magical days and magnificent experiences. The more you jump in and take on challenges together, even the puky ones, that's when God is glorified the most and also when you'll find your marriage the most satisfying. It's then you'll have the best shot at finding happiness.

The upside of marriage will exceed your most exquisite dreams. God is the master at cleaning up others' messes. Jesus gave up *everything* for us, and it's when we imitate Jesus that we find the greatest joy. Especially in marriage.

Which brings us back to that oh-so-critical question: *Why* are you getting married? The most important question you need to ask yourself is: Are you ready to serve this person for the rest of your life? That's right, *SERVE*! Puke and all? Think about that for a minute, and let it sink in.

If you are entering into this marriage because of what you will *get*, believe me, you will be gravely disappointed. (Again with the puke.) But, on the other hand, if you are entering into it for what you can *give*, then—aha!—you are starting to get it.

Marriage is about giving. Giving unselfishly. If you've been told that marriage is fifty-fifty, think again. Going into marriage with a fifty-fifty mindset will set you on a course for a doomsday disaster.

Do me a favor and just look at the divorce rate. Want to talk about a fifty-fifty split? Go sit in on a *Him vs. Her* divorce court case and you'll witness two once-madly-in-love people with their lawyers, standing before a judge fighting over money, the house, and splitting the kids. You may have already experienced this yourself and are now vowing to never do it again.

I once went to court in support of a friend who was getting a divorce, and I was overwhelmed with indescribable sadness. I sat in the courtroom with tears in my eyes and my heart in my stomach, watching my dear friend and her husband fight it out through their lawyers. She was on one side and he was on the other, both miserable with discontent and angst-filled about the impending outcome. The lawyers spoke for them, and it felt like a fight no one could ever win. And all this before a judge who, I might add, didn't know either of them or their children. All I've got to say is: Case closed.

Never settle for fifty-fifty. You've got to give it your *all*.

## The Marriage Manual

God will do beyond our highest hopes and fantasy dreams if we allow Him to, if we submit to the marriage He describes in the Bible. "Now to Him who is able to do far more abundantly beyond all that we ask or think, according to the power that works within us, to Him be the glory in the church and in Christ Jesus to all generations forever and ever. Amen" (Ephesians 3:20–21). When we follow what God says about marriage, He will work miracles in our relationships. God created marriage, and the Bible contains the manual for a happy, thriving marriage. It's up to you to follow it or not.

First things first, you need to examine your hearts according to 2 Corinthians 6:14: "Do not be bound together with unbelievers; for what partnership have righteousness and lawlessness, or what fellowship has light with darkness?" Is your betrothed a believer? Does he or she love the Lord? How about you? Are you committed to Jesus Christ as Lord? If one of you is a Christian and the other is not, I urge you to call it off. You'd be signing up for a whole lot of hurt and problems.

Men, look at Ephesians 5:28: "So husbands ought also to love their own wives as their own bodies. He who loves his own wife loves himself." Men, are you ready to make a commitment such as this?

Ready, ladies? Are you ready to hop on his train? Consider Ephesians 5:22: "Wives, *be subject* to your own husbands, as to the Lord" (emphasis added). How are you both going to work out that verse as a couple? Anyone fighting yet?

If either of you is pointing fingers, point one back at

yourself. Happy marriages are the ones where couples look at themselves and work at being the best spouse they can be. You can't change your partner, but you can change *you*. If you think you're going to change him or her after you get married, change your direction and march back home. Decide today you will love your beloved with all of your being and focus on his or her God-given assets and not faults.

If you've determined not to be another divorce statistic, know that the beginning of your marriage and the physical, emotional, and spiritual relationship with your spouse is the start of something wonderful, something incredibly magnificent. It's like when you first became a Christian. You weren't sure what was ahead, but you knew it would be something great. Beyond what words could describe. Whatever happens, you will tackle it as a team.

## Exposed

...Which brings me to the topic I know you're already thinking about. In fact, you've probably skimmed over chapter nine already. That's good! Briefly, you are about to embark on a journey as husband and wife and as most cherished friends, but you are embarking on a sexual excursion as well. Sex can be one of the best parts of your marriage journey, one that will get better and better with each individual voyage. Some cruises will be smooth sailing, some windy, others stormy, some really rocky, and some will blow you away! Welcome them all and embrace each one.

There will be days when one of you will not feel like

"sailing"; what are you going to do then?

Entering into a marriage covenant is saying you are willing to give yourself to this person emotionally, spiritually, *and* physically. If you're not prepared to have an ongoing, active sexual relationship with your future husband or wife, think twice about getting married. I'm not kidding. If you don't plan on making your sexual relationship a priority, consider remaining friends. Eat ice cream together and watch a fireworks show.

Strong marriages have strong "fireworks" of their own. If you're not willing to work in this area and all areas of intimacy (emotional and spiritual), then you're being grossly unfair to the man or woman you claim to adore. (Remind yourself of this ten years and multiple kids down the road!)

You are about to commit to a *forever* union that will not only seal you together as one but will chisel you into a masterpiece for God. Marriage will chip away the rough edges. Your faults and shortcomings will be just as exposed as your bodies. Every selfish part of you, every ounce of pride, every negative word or deed will become evident. The worst parts of you will spill out all over the one you vowed to love forever. (Think puke on a cruise ship.) You either have to put your selfish desires to death, or your selfishness will put your marriage to death.

*His* mistakes become *your* mistakes. This also means *her* ugly parts will spill on *you*. How are you going to respond when your spouse barks at you or, worse, yells at you? How are you going to respond when he or she seems to hurt your feelings on purpose? How are you going to handle feelings of rejection because your spouse doesn't feel like talking or having sex?

I know you're thinking, *Oh, not us! We get along great! We are soul mates! We totally love each other! We can't wait to begin our sex life!*

Those are the exact words of almost every couple who has pranced down the aisle. Many who are no longer together. Many who now say, "We just don't love each other anymore. My spouse changed. We grew apart. I wasn't happy."

But here's a secret all successful married couples know: Marriage isn't about you. It's not about you being happy or your spouse being happy. Yes, extreme joy and happiness can be a by-product of marriage—that's the way God designed it. In order to obtain the kind of marriage that honors God, you must fight against your innate selfish nature. When everything inside of you screams *I need to take care of ME and look out for ME.* You have to exchange *ME* thinking for *WE* thinking. You need to bury self-centered thinking and think in terms of what is best for your relationship and new family.

When you honor your spouse, you honor God. Your marriage can be a tool God can use to point people to *Him* when you have a God-centered marriage. It is through giving in marriage that you will get the greatest joy. Marriage at its best is two people loving each other selflessly. When loving unconditionally and selflessly can be mastered, your union can feel like heaven. It can blow your mind. It can feel like you're living a dream. The key to this begins with allowing God to mold you.

Right now, putting the other first feels easy because you're both putting your best forward. Reading this book indicates you desire to continue in your quest to always be the best wife/husband you can. At this point in your journey, the more prepared you are, the better. There are so many books on this subject because it is so vitally important. You can't be overprepared. Soak it all in. And then, after you're married, don't ever stop learning.

## Never Forget Your Courtship

Your wedding day will be a very abnormal day. Nothing in life will be quite like it. In the morning, you wake up a single person, and by the end of the day you will be a husband or a wife.

One of the biggest tips I can give you at this point is to tell you to *remember your courtship*. Even after the wedding bells have quieted, remember how you always looked good for him. Remember how you brought her flowers and opened doors for her. Make a mental note of how you treat each other—journal your courtship even. The way you treat your spouse-to-be now, continue doing so from your wedding day on. Each day, try to treat each other better than the day before. When you stop treating him or her as well as you do now, that will be the start of the downfall of your marriage.

Do you want to feel madly in love *throughout* your marriage. . .just like you feel today? This is the secret ingredient: Always treat your spouse as you do today or even better. Even when you don't feel like it! Take out the trash for her when you see it overflowing. Make him his favorite dessert, just because. Or better yet, *be* his favorite dessert. Let her

18

know if you'll be coming home late. What seem like small kindnesses will grow your marriage stronger and stronger.

For example, I fall in love with my husband over and over. Do you want to know why? There are many big things he does for me, but truthfully, it's the "small things" that cause me to fall in love with him *all over again*.

As I write this, I'm thinking back to yesterday. I was in my office typing away and had left our bed half-made. After washing the sheets, I got distracted and never finished making our bed. Walking through our bedroom, I noticed my husband had finished my undone bed project. Tears welled up in my eyes as I saw his kind act of love. My next move was to go and thank him. It was no big deal to him, but for me, I fell in love with him *all over again*.

Never stop showing acts of love and kindness. Never stop rescuing her. Never stop being his cheerleader. Never stop looking for ways to lift her up. Never stop complimenting him.

When my husband and I first got married, we didn't understand the concept of putting the other first. We were both looking out for "me." As you can imagine, *we* fought almost constantly. The more we tried to get *all we wanted*, the worse our marriage became. It wasn't until we both became Christians—five years into our marriage—that we began building a marriage we could honor God with.

When you learn to clean up vomit with a servant's heart, life will be better than you ever imagined possible. It's time to put "we" before "me."

# Discussion Questions

- Have people been telling you that marriage is hard? If so, how do you feel about this?

- Why do you want to get married? What feelings come up when you hear that question? Discuss what your dreams and desires for marriage are.

- If you had a marriage like your parents, would that be good or bad? Why? (See chapter eight for more on this.)

- What will serving your spouse look like to you? Is the idea of *giving* to the other person instead of *getting* a new concept for you?

- Do you think of marriage as fifty-fifty? Where might you be tempted to fall into this trap?

- What constitutes an act of kindness to you? What makes you feel loved?

- Look for married couples you would like to emulate. Discuss what you see in their marriage that seems desirable to you. Take the discussion to another level and make appointments to ask these couples questions about why they seem so happy together.

# Chapter Two
## Don't Make It about the Ceremony

The invitations to the wedding were all addressed and stuffed in the pretty envelopes, tucked in with the fancy writing and elegant decor.

"Ummm, Monica, did you notice the misspelled word?" Our only daughter was to be married in less than two months and *Mom* had to open her big mouth! In my own defense—it wasn't just *any* misspelled word—it was our last name. On the first line of all 120 stylish wedding invitations, *Williams* was spelled W-i-l-l-a-m-s. It read: *Mike and Lucille Willams request the honor...*

It just sort of slipped out. I should have said nothing. But of course, I couldn't do that. In all of my years after taking the name Williams, I had never seen it misspelled. My maiden name had been misspelled plenty. *Recenello.* Say that ten times! Or even once. I welcomed my new name and loved that people knew how to say it and spell it. That is...up until my daughter's wedding invitations were all done and ready to be mailed.

My daughter said, "Oh well, that's not what matters most anyway. No one will care." Actually, *NO*, that is *NOT* how it went at all!

Here's the truth: She screamed, "NOOOOOO!" and dramatically dropped her head into her hands and cried inconsolably for thirty minutes. I felt terrible. Her groom did everything he knew to try and comfort her. Yeah, I should have kept my mouth shut!

But do you want to know something? I was the only one who noticed. All the invitations went out, and not one person said a single word about it. I waited for the fun-hearted jokes, but no one seemed to notice, or care about the massacre of our last name. Later I even asked a few friends, and not one person recognized our name slaughtering. How about that?

Now our Willams debacle is just a funny story to tell around a campfire. At the end of the walk down the aisle, it didn't make one bit of difference!

## The Preparations Can Make You Crazy

I am well aware of the fact that weddings take a lot of planning and arranging. And someone has to do all the work. Are you working together?

Ladies, some men love to be involved in the process, while others would rather focus on the honeymoon. Whichever man you have, be thankful for him. This is an exercise in being grateful for the man he is.

Men, does she need help? After all, it is your wedding, too. Find ways to assist her.

Weddings are a group effort, and working as a team will help set the foundation for your married life together.

You are forming a *Forever Team*. The most important team you'll ever belong to. Learn how to be a good team player. What does a good team player look like? A good team player gives their best effort. He communicates when he's feeling overwhelmed and needing a break. She understands when her teammate has differing opinions and desires, realizing her "Top Ten Critical Tasks" list may not make it on his.

Men and women are very different, and now is the time to recognize the vast difference. You will not always approach situations in the same manner; get used to this. God has designed boys and girls uniquely diverse.

Wander over to a playground. Watch how the boys play compared with how the girls play. The boys are loud and running. The girls are probably sitting down with another little girl talking or moving along in a *togetherness* group. He is still the little boy who wants to run. She still wants to talk and connect and feel like part of a group. He wants to connect, too, but he'll connect differently. He may or may not care about what color the dresses are, but he cares about you and wants you to be happy. Have you ever noticed it seems to be the little boys who run back to Mom? "Mommy, did you see me jump?" "Mommy, watch me swing!" "Mommy, look how fast I can run!" For a little boy, part of the fun and allure of a playground is to show off his *skills*. Boys—men—have a deep desire to connect; they just do it in their own way. Ladies, never forget this. He is not like you. He will prepare for the wedding vastly different than you will.

My husband had only one request regarding our wedding day. He didn't want me to wear a veil over my face when I walked down the aisle. Easy enough, right? You would think so, but for me it was one of the most agonizing decisions I made during my wedding planning process.

I'll tell you why. My mother was extremely invested in the idea of my wearing a veil *over* my face. Extremely. For some reason it mattered to her greatly. Perhaps she, too, had thought about this special day when her daughter would be married and *did exactly as she had* and walked down the aisle with a veiled face. She brought it up numerous times and petitioned for a veil-covered face, even though my betrothed had requested the opposite.

I was stuck in a huge quandary. I sincerely wanted to make my mom happy, but I also wanted to do what my future husband had asked, especially since this was his only request. What do you think I did? What would you do? Maybe I should have pulled the veil forward and cut a big hole for my face. Debatably, that would have been a compromise. Yet, this situation was not a time for compromise. It was a time to set a pace for my future marriage.

I did not wear the veil over my face. But you need to know—being a people pleaser, wanting to keep *everyone* happy—it wasn't easy at all.

As I walked down the aisle it was a symbol to Mike, the love of my life, my protector and covering: "I'm on your team. You are my number one. Now and forever."

The wedding day needs to be about showing each other and the world that you have become a team of two.

## Strengthening Your Union

During your courtship, begin taking the steps to shout to the world, "We are a dynamic duo!" You will not be able to keep everyone happy. Each challenge stands as an opportunity to act as a unified front. With every decision, consider your future spouse and how it will make him feel. Consider her feelings while making choices about your first night together as husband and wife.

Talk through all of your wedding decisions. Listen for feelings. How? Always approach each conversation trying to understand where the other person is coming from and why they feel as they do. This simple step will prevent many arguments. Ask yourself, "How would I feel if I were in his/her shoes?" Understand the situation from their point of view. Ask questions to understand, not to contest. Then listen. *Listen.* Listen to understand. Now is a good time to exercise the advice in James 1:19, "…everyone must be quick to hear, slow to speak and slow to anger."

## Uniting Two Families

Be mindful how family members can unintentionally make hurtful comments.

When my oldest son was in college and driving distance away, I'd visit him usually once a week. I would leave early in the morning and drive through two hours of traffic in order to spend the day with him. I loved and cherished the days we got to spend together. (Yes, I'm guilty of being *that* kind of mom!) During the time he was engaged and living in another state, I traveled to visit him. I so desperately wanted to re-create a mother-son college-day reunion. Finally, when his day off arrived, he informed me his fiancée would be joining us.

Without thinking, I foolishly said, "But I thought it was going to be just you and me."

My son was quick to respond, "Mom, suck it up! She is going to be my wife. She's coming with us."

Instantly, I apologized and wished I could roll up the words like a vacuum hose and put them back.

I immediately felt ashamed for saying what I did. Think about it: I was about to get a new daughter, and she wanted to spend time with me. What a precious gem of a young lady. And so true to who she remains to this day. Jenny has been one of the greatest blessings in my life and the *greatest* blessing in my son's life. It was quite unwise and careless of me to say what I did. It's on my list of top ten stupid things I've ever said.

You need to understand this process can create quite an adjustment for your parents. Especially moms of sons. I'm not exactly sure why, but throughout my years it has proven to be true. Could it be because it's a "little boy's" last giant step away from Mom? Give your mom time to get used to the new dynamics. Ladies, don't take offense when your future mother-in-law spouts off reckless ramblings. Even the best of us have said really stupid stuff!

Do you have a close relationship with your mom? This is a good thing, but Mom absolutely needs to move to number two. What does this look like? Consider your future wife first in everything. Her feelings need to come before Mom's feelings. Don't tell Mom anything your fiancée wouldn't want said.

Is it time to start setting some boundaries with your mother? Is it time to begin to let everyone know that your future wife is your number one?

Ladies, how close are you to Dad? My daughter was, and still is, extremely close to her dad. On Monica's wedding day, as she and her dad approached "the handoff," they waited for the cue from the wedding coordinator for the bride to begin her descent down the white carpet. The wedding processional had already traveled down the aisle, and all eyes were looking for the bride. They got the awaited signal to go.

Mike asked, "Are you ready?"

She firmly said, "No!"

"Okay, we'll wait here." Mike says he would have walked her as far away as she wanted if she had requested.

He prayed for her.

Monica waited a couple of seconds and took a few deep breaths. "Okay, I'm ready."

She was very nervous. Not about marrying Kyle. . .she was sure about that from the beginning of their courtship. She was nervous about being the center of attention. Her dad completely understood this. Her dad completely understood *her*.

"The handoff" signifies a change. You go from Dad to your husband. You now go to your husband first. You think of him above all others. What he thinks matters more than what Dad thinks. Every time Monica goes to her dad for advice, the first words out of my husband's mouth are "What does Kyle think?" If you're used to going to Dad for advice and comfort, begin to transfer your requisitions to your future husband. This does not mean you stop going to your dad for wise counsel; it means you decide *together* when to go to Dad. You never want your husband to feel second to your dad.

And ladies, you want to avoid statements such as, "My mom and I think. . ." No, no, no. In his mind he's thinking, *Now I have to deal with her and her mom?* Never give him the idea you and your mom are a united front opposing him. How would that make him feel?

This is what your relationship lineup looks like after marriage: God, spouse. . .then, numbers three and four can fluctuate depending on your season of life—i.e., children or ailing parents. But even after number three gets filled in with babies, your spouse remains your top human relationship.

Again, consider how the Bible instructs us in Ephesians 5:31: "For this reason a man shall leave his father and mother and shall be joined to his wife, and the two shall become one flesh." In no other human relationship does God instruct us to *cleave*. Let's look at the definition of the word according to Dictionary.com: to adhere closely; stick; cling; to remain faithful.

In other words, stuck like glue! After you say "I do," you are stuck like glue. Does the notion of being "stuck like glue" to another sound appealing to you? The wedding process will give you a very real glimpse into what your life together will be like. If this process is *all about me*, you are setting a foundation of selfishness for your marriage.

## The Perfect Day

Is your goal to achieve *The Perfect Day*?

As you scuffle through to "your perfect day," consider

what the cost will be along the way with such a purpose in mind. Did you damage relationships in the process? Did you damage your most important relationship? If you turn into a Bridezilla or a Groomzilla, basically what you're saying is your wedding is all about *you*.

Girls, especially, are taught from a very young age: "This day is all about you." It is not. Not!

One bride had her wedding dress ruined during the alteration process. That will put a glitch in your magical day! After her dream dress had been damaged, she had no choice but to settle on a dress she could find in time. It wasn't her first choice, but she didn't allow a dress to deter her from the delight of marrying the love of her life.

Jamie, busy with graduate school, purchased her perfect wedding dress from a bridal show. Since the dress needed to be cleaned, she found a dry cleaner with a good reputation for cleaning wedding dresses. A week before her wedding, Jamie's mom picked up the dress for her. Jamie was home studying when her mom called her.

"Sweetheart, I have some bad news."

"Okay, what is it? Just tell me, Mom."

"Well. . .umm. . .your dress is ruined."

"Define *ruined*."

"Well. . .it looks to be a smoky gray, and the lace is damaged, and it looks like it shrunk."

"Okay, well, let me finish studying and we can deal with this later."

Jamie didn't freak out! Listening to her tell the story, I expected some kind of explosion, but she remained oddly calm

29

during her dress crisis. She ended up finding the same dress from a private seller across the country, and they shipped it to her just in time. And the smoky gray dress, Jamie used that one for wedding pictures *in* the ocean. Her wedding was on the beach, and jumping into the water for pictures was a natural thing to do when you had an extra *damaged* dress.

Gentlemen, preparations can get stressful for you as well, so talk with your soon-to-be bride about any concerns or anxiety, and keep focused on building a foundation to begin your life as husband and wife.

Think in terms of your *whole life*. Not just *one day*!

Your wedding day begins your journey as husband and wife. How do you want to begin this journey? Striving to achieve one perfect day? It's much better to springboard from a foundation of grace, teamwork, trust, and togetherness.

A great marriage is about two people yielding to each other. The wedding day, and preparations, can look the same. Start your family centered around love, respect, and honor.

We think the pictures and the cake and the colors and the venue and the food and the dress and the invitations. . . *and. . .and. . .and. . .*are critically important. Straight up, if you asked me to show you my wedding pictures, it would take me a while to find my wedding album. I can't even remember what we ate at our wedding reception or what the cake looked like. I can't remember what our invitations said or what color they were. I can't remember who our photographer was or if I even liked him.

I do remember the color of the bridesmaids' dresses because it was my mom's choice and the same color she had at her wedding. And you know what, I'm glad it made her happy. Because today I couldn't care less what color my bridal party wore. And I didn't care much on the day of my wedding either.

I can also remember the color the groomsmen wore. I remember because I thought it was strange. They wore white. My husband and his best man thought it was cool. And more importantly, I remember how they beamed with pride as they told me the color—or *non-color*—they had chosen. They were very happy. I thought choosing white was weird. Okay. Who cares? It doesn't make one bit of difference today.

I'm not at all saying these things don't have a place. I understand your wedding day debuts as a big deal, but don't give nonessentials top billing. Only your beloved can hold that place. And the way you treat each other through this process matters. The foundation you establish will reach into the next ten years. . .thirty years. . .fifty years. . .and maybe even more.

Let me share with you what did matter most on our wedding day: it mattered that we honored each other and were a united front.

When the minister said we could kiss, we didn't make out in front of my grandmother. *Why does the kiss matter?* Keeping the kiss classy shows respect for each other and family. A pastor once told me that while he was officiating a wedding and announced, "You may kiss the bride," the couple went at it like two cows French kissing. This pastor felt *uncomfortable*, to say the least.

Slobbering can be saved for later. Go ahead and slobber,

drool, devour, ingest each other—later, behind closed doors. Grandma doesn't want to see that.

We stuck together—like glue—at our reception. *It's only one day. . . . Why does sticking together matter?* At a wedding my husband officiated I noticed the groom seemed to spend more time with his mother than his new bride during the fancy reception, at a fancy hotel. Yikes! Everything seemed fancy except the bride and groom's connection. Your wedding day begins your life as a couple, a family. Pay more attention to your spouse than anyone else. Begin by putting your number one *as number one.*

We didn't smear cake all over each other. *The cake? Really?* Yes! Watching cake fly and be smeared all over might be fun, but how does this establish confidence and trust? Ladies, show respect for your man. Guys, when the crowd screams for you to throw cake at her, don't do it! This is the first test on trust. Pass it.

Allow me to break this down for you. Your relationship and how you treat your future spouse is what's most import-ant. Establishing "us" over "I." "We" comes before "me."

"Our wedding went perfectly." I have never heard those words. Ever. Have you? If anyone out there can say that, please contact me.

You can't have the perfect day. *Stuff* happens.

You *can* have a better day. Exceedingly better. You can have a day that will set you up for success in your marriage. Rather than focusing on one day, focus on the rest of your life. Isn't a marriage filled with contentment, mutual respect, and honor for God a more noble goal? Look toward the long-range objective. When you become other-centered, and long-term focused, little disturbances along the way will fall into their proper place. As challenges arise, tackle each as opportunities to be united as a couple.

Mistakes, debacles, mishaps—which turn into funny stories—will make your marriage stronger. Look at each other and say, "Another funny story to tell later; we are getting stronger." As you embark on many years together, focus on trust, honor, respect, and loving each other. Challenges, struggles, and faux pas will strengthen your relationship and cement you together. Like glue.

# Discussion Questions

- Have you been striving toward a goal of "The Perfect Day"? Do you think this goal is realistic?

- What does a successful wedding look like to you? Discuss what your desires are for this big day.

- What does the phrase "stuck like glue" mean to you? How does that make you feel?

- How do you expect to feel the day after your wedding day? Discuss your answer.

- Who is doing most of the work regarding the preparation and planning of your wedding? Are you both happy with this arrangement? Do you need to include him more? Do you need to step up and help her more?

- Do you think this process will make your relationship stronger? What needs to happen for you both to stay unified during this process?

# Chapter Three
## Forgiveness

As a child, I grew up in a home with a dad who told me there was no God. I can remember conversations about the nonexistence of God as early as I learned how to form words.

Dad made it very clear: "When you're dead, you're dead. You didn't know anything before you got here, and you won't know anything after you leave here."

As you can imagine, this message was hard to process as a child. Most nights all I could think about was *I'm going to be dead someday. Dead for many, many, many years.* It was frightening. My little heart raced.

I grew up believing my dad wholeheartedly. I accepted his proposal that there was no God and adjusted to the gnawing feeling of utter emptiness. I had no hope. No purpose. Bad decisions didn't seem to have consequences. Nothing seemed to matter. And yet, there was a deep desire in my heart that was unquenchable. I rectified my yearnings with the assumption that when I got married—and really felt acceptance and love, along with a home and career—the empty space would be filled. Disappointingly, after marriage my heart ached even more. Any hope I had was shattered.

The emptiness multiplied as the years added up. Five years

into my marriage, the world I had created around me was broken. I hated my marriage. I hated my life. I hated myself. There was no forgiveness in my heart for others or myself. Beginning the process of a search for something more, I began reading the Bible along with books about Jesus.

Pondering the obscure notion of even a slender possibility of Dad being wrong about God, I asked him a question one day.

"Dad, I know you don't believe in God, but what do you believe about Jesus?"

What he said blew my mind. I remember it like it was yesterday even though it was over twenty-five years ago. "Jesus was here; that's historical fact."

"What? You believe Jesus was here? What do you believe about Him?"

"He got down off the cross and went to China." Dad believed Jesus was some sort of biblical-day magician.

Come again? I could hardly believe what I was hearing. For me, to believe that Jesus Christ was the Son of God and died for us made a million times more sense than He was an ancient-day David Copperfield. Shortly after, I received God's forgiveness, recognized Jesus Christ as Lord of my life, and accepted Him into my life.

Like only God can orchestrate, Mike and I became Christians a day apart from each other. A young pastor and his wife moved into our condominium complex and befriended us. I had a desire to attend church but wouldn't go without my husband. At first Mike was adamantly opposed to the idea. I told God it had to be both of us; I wouldn't go without my husband. And so, I waited. Until one day our friend Dave wanted to date one of my friends. Knowing she was a Christian, I informed Dave she would only date him if he went to church. (I understand now that it's not about going to church but having a relationship with the God of the universe, but at the time I thought all Dave had to do was go to church.) Dave was reluctant, but Mike said, "If you go, I'll go." However, when Sunday morning rolled around, Dave backed out. Having already committed to going to church, Mike and I went. I'll have you know he was *not* happy about it though, complaining all the way there. On that particular day we did not have a good church experience, and after arriving home, Mike suggested we try the church our young pastor friends attended. We ended up going on a regular basis.

Separately, God began to work in each of our hearts. Until one day I was at the gym and decided I wanted to follow Jesus Christ. I knew He was real, that He lived a sinless life, died for me, and that I needed to accept His free gift of eternal life. When I arrived home, alone, I got down on my knees and asked Jesus to come into my life and be the boss, the Master, my Savior. I told no one. Not even my husband. Two weeks later I was talking on the phone with my sister proclaiming I had made a decision to follow Jesus, prompting her to do the same. Mike interjected that he had, too. I told my sister, "And Mike has, too." After getting off the phone, Mike and I looked at each other. "You?" "Yes." "You?" "Yes." "When?" It was a day apart from each other two weeks earlier. God. Is. Good. From the moment I decided to follow Jesus, I've felt forgiven, loved, and accepted. The moment I gave my life over to the One who created and loved me, my life has been changed and redefined. Shame no longer seized me; fear of death turned into joy for living eternally with my heavenly Father. My life took on a whole new meaning.

The Bible tells us "that if you confess with your mouth Jesus as Lord, and believe in your heart that God raised Him from the dead, you will be saved; for with the heart a person believes, resulting in righteousness, and with the mouth he confesses, resulting in salvation" (Romans 10:9–10).

After I met the God of all forgiveness and love, my whole world changed. I changed. Forgiving others became easy after accepting how I had been forgiven.

Have you felt God's love and forgiveness? It's never too late to receive God's mercy and confess Jesus Christ as Lord. In order to have the best marriage you can possibly have, taking the step of accepting Jesus, receiving forgiveness, and proclaiming Him as Lord will offer you the optimum platform for a thriving, loving, and fulfilling marriage.

## Setting the Stage for a Thriving Marriage

Never forget that forgiveness started with God, the Creator and sustainer of life, who created all things. *All things.* Including forgiveness. He first forgave us.

When it comes to forgiveness, there is no better place to begin than the Bible. Let's take a look at what Jesus said after He answered Peter's question about forgiveness and instructed us to forgive "seventy times seven" times (Matthew 18:22):

*"For this reason the kingdom of heaven may be compared to a king who wished to settle accounts with his slaves. When he had begun to settle them, one who owed him ten thousand talents was brought to him. But since he did not have the means to repay, his lord commanded him to be sold, along with his wife and children and all that he had, and repayment to be made. So the slave fell to the ground and prostrated himself before him, saying, 'Have patience with me and I will repay you everything.' And the lord of that slave felt compassion and released him and forgave him the debt. But that slave went out and found one of his fellow slaves who owed him a hundred denarii; and he seized him and began to choke him, saying, 'Pay back what you owe.' So his fellow slave fell to the ground and began to plead with him, saying, 'Have patience with me and I will repay you.' But he was unwilling and went and threw him in prison until he should pay back what was owed. So when his fellow slaves saw what had happened, they were deeply grieved and came and reported to their lord all that had happened. Then summoning him, his lord said to him, 'You wicked slave, I forgave you all that debt because you pleaded with me. Should you not also have had mercy on your fellow slave, in the same way that I had mercy on you?' And his lord, moved with anger, handed him over to the torturers until he should repay*

*all that was owed him. My heavenly Father will also
do the same to you, if each of you does not forgive his
brother from your heart."*
—Matthew 18:23–35

Mark the above passage in your Bible. Read it often throughout your marriage, especially when your feelings have been hurt. Don't underestimate the influence hurt feelings can have. You *will* get your feelings hurt; count on it. Be prepared. The best way to ward off an attack is to be ready. *Wow, slow down. You're making this sound like war!* Trust me, after your feelings have been hurt, it will feel like war.

*"A happy marriage is the union of two forgivers."*
—Ruth Bell Graham

Many people look at forgiveness as something we do for the other person. While this does help others along their forgiveness journey, the main reason we need to forgive others is for ourselves. As we just read, the unforgiving person was handed over to the torturers. *He* was the one being tortured. When we fail to release another for hurting us, *we* torture ourselves. Did you catch that? When you harbor bitterness in your heart, you willingly put yourself in your own created prison. Self-punishment is a very cruel form of torture. Don't do it. And don't do it to your marriage. It's like putting "we" in prison.

When you refuse to forgive, it puts your marriage in

prison. Putting *WE* before *ME* includes a heart free from bitterness and grudges toward each other and others. Bitterness spews out in many nasty ways. In order to have the best marriage, the one God intends for you, you *must* clear your heart of all resentment and anger toward those who have hurt you—starting with your future spouse. You want to begin your marriage with a clean slate. A clean heart.

There will be plenty of hurt feelings as your years together build up; you want a heart free from resentment on the day you say "I do." I know it's hard to believe now how years together can increase hurt feelings. Right now you're filled with elated emotions as you enter your new life as a couple. The stark truth is the deeper you love, the deeper the possibility for wounds.

The first time I felt deeply hurt by my then–new husband, I felt like our marriage was over and my world was coming to an end. Sounds a bit dramatic, huh? Tell that to my young heart! At the time it didn't feel dramatic at all. My world was ending! I felt confused and filled with deep despair. I didn't know what to do with the hurt, and I didn't know how to fix it, either. Which brings me to the purpose of this chapter: how to prevent built-up resentment in your marriage, and what to do when you've been hurt or when you've caused hurt.

*"Only the brave know how to forgive. A coward never forgives. It's not in his nature."*
—Robert Muller

For some of you, just by reading this, it cuts open scars and brings up deep-seated wounds from your past. You may have been abused, suffered a huge loss, or gone through severe trauma. Forgiveness may seem like a mountain too monstrous to climb. Give yourself time to warm up. Stretch your legs, buy new hiking boots, and then begin to climb that mountain—when you're ready. But don't ignore it. This mountain of hurt will divide you and your future spouse if you neglect to tackle it.

I have a close friend, Mary (not her real name; most names have been changed throughout this book), who, after twenty years of marriage and three children, called me from a locked room in her home.

"Lucille, I've locked myself in the spare room in our house. I've been drinking, and Larry said if I get drunk like this again, he's leaving me."

I am happy to report Mary joined AA, got a sponsor, and has been sober for over three years. But all of the hurts and buried anger and resentment came to a head one night after Mary locked herself in a room. She was forced to face it or lose everything she held dear. I am so proud of her for being brave enough to embrace the painful road of recovery.

Mary had some deep hurts she had never addressed, and it spewed out as a drinking problem. When we get together and share what's happening in our lives, there's a phrase she repeats to me often. As we talk through struggles, disappointments, and the normal challenges of life, I'll hear it over and over. Mary says, "I can't have resentment. I'm not allowed." She keeps her heart clear of bitterness and resentment. Toward *anyone*. I've done my best to adopt this motto as well.

To understand this mantra more fully, I decided to sit in a room with those who know how to forgive. In fact, their future success depends on it. I went to an Alcoholics Anonymous (AA) meeting. It was my first time, and I attended with Mary, who regularly decrees, "I'm not allowed to have resentment." In a room full of expert forgivers I felt like an imposter and feared being rejected by this open, women-only, AA group.

To my delight, I was welcomed and embraced there more than any other group meeting I have ever attended. They were the definition of loving and accepting. I sincerely felt loved and accepted for just being me. And the only two words I uttered were "Hello" and "Lu." When each woman spoke, she focused on what she had done wrong and how she could fully forgive those who had hurt or offended her; and she expressed love and support for everyone in the room. I wanted to jump up and scream, "YES! YES! YES!" But I stuck with "Hello" and "Lu."

No resentment allowed.

Decide right now there will be no resentment allowed in your marriage. Make a pact today establishing an overriding peace treaty with a decree of NO RESENTMENT ALLOWED. This starts with a decision to always forgive, *before* you have an offense to forgive. Be secure in knowing you will be forgiven and that you will offer forgiveness to your spouse.

When we are loved and accepted for who we are, and forgiven unconditionally, we are free to be the best version of ourselves. Your marriage will take on the best version of marriage possible.

Even after over thirty-four years of marriage, forgiveness remains at the forefront of our marriage. Do you have any idea how difficult it might be to write about marriage and forgiveness when you've recently "had words" or been hurt by your spouse? I have to fix it. And fast!

Very recently, Mike and I were hurrying to leave for church. Yes, church! When I finished getting ready and walked into the kitchen, he was cleaning the dishes. What I should have said was, "Thank you for getting those dishes done." But I didn't. Instead, I asked him for assistance with something I needed. (Now, a smarter woman would have left him alone to finish!) Well, as you can imagine, he barked.

I'm sure he felt unappreciated—*but I wasn't looking at the situation from his view*—all I could think about was how I was feeling at the "offense" I had endured. Being very sensitive (and, guys, most women are!), it hurt my feelings. It hurt my feelings a lot.

On the ride to church I talked about how I felt. It went like this: "It really hurt my feelings when you barked at me. Perhaps I picked a bad time, but I didn't deserve the way you talked to me. I feel sad and I want to withdraw." At the end I added, "You're not on my top ten favorite people list right now." I know, I know, I could have left my last comment out. For some reason, I felt really wounded by our unfriendly kitchen exchange and I needed him to know.

After expressing how I felt and hearing how he felt, I was

able to clear my heart of resentment and fill it back up with love for him. Whether or not we apologized, even though we *both* did, didn't matter. Listening to his viewpoint, I was able to fully grasp how discounted and unappreciated he felt, and getting my feelings out paved the way to a heart free of bitterness.

When I think of all the times my husband has forgiven me, it becomes easier to forgive him. If you're going to keep a record, don't keep a record of times you've had to forgive your spouse. Keep a record of how many times your spouse has forgiven you.

Which brings me to a time I had to ask my husband for his forgiveness. I had breached a confidence Mike trusted me with—one of the worst things you can do as a pastor's wife. I thought it would help a hurting friend, and I made a huge misjudgment call. Certain of the repercussions of my misstep, I knew I needed to come clean with my husband. I decided I was going to drive to Mike's office, confess the trust I had broken, and ask for his forgiveness. I knew he would forgive me, but I was still scared. And I fully expected him to be mad at me. He had every right to be.

As I was getting ready, I sobbed, completely distraught by my own actions. Suddenly the phone rang. It was Mike. My plan was to answer, hide my distress, finish getting ready, and head out to talk with him in person. I don't hide things well. He detected "hidden" panic in my voice. When he asked me what was wrong, I broke down with gasping cries. I told him what I had done and asked for his forgiveness. What he said soothed me like aloe to a burn. He said, "Honey, I forgive you. It's okay; we'll get through this together."

How in the world can I ever be mad at a man who forgives like that?

If you want a marriage with unconditional love, acceptance, and forgiveness, you must offer unconditional love, acceptance, and forgiveness. Forgiving an offense does not mean you condone wrongdoing. It means you will not hold it against the other person. What I did was still wrong, but he didn't retaliate or treat me any differently because of it.

I can honestly say I have not made the same mistake again in breaching a confidence. Mike's forgiveness, understanding, and trust paved the way for me to be a better person. His love freed me to be a new and improved version of me. Which makes for a better version of *WE*.

Resentment can creep in and take a foothold, even in the best of marriages. Brad, happily married for fifteen years with two girls and his first boy on the way, talked with me about this very subject. He told me he had mild bitterness in his heart toward his wife. It had been building up over many years, and he'd never addressed it nor felt like he could address it, especially now because of his wife's pregnancy. "It's built up little by little, and now I have resentment in my heart toward her. I don't know what to do with it. I know it's hurting our marriage."

First, I think Brad was being prudent in waiting for the right opportunity to talk with his wife. Rushing into serious conversations can be damaging. Choosing the right time to talk can be just as important as having the conversation.

An example of this principle is Queen Esther in the

Bible. When Esther learned of Haman, a trusted adviser to her husband, King Ahasuerus, having a plan of annihilating her people, the Jews, the first thing she did was to go to God.

One would think Esther would immediately run to her husband and tell him of Haman's plot. She did not. She fasted and prayed.

You might then think as soon as Esther was done praying, she would run to her husband and request he do something about the devious schemes of Haman. But she didn't.

Instead Esther invited the king and Haman to a banquet she prepared. She displayed love, honor, and respect. While they were eating and drinking, the king asked Esther what her request was. Esther requested the king and Haman return the next day for another banquet. She showed her husband *double* honor and respect. You can read the full story in the book of Esther, chapters 3–7.

After the second banquet, the king asked yet again what was Esther's request. Listen to the beautiful way she asked: "Then Queen Esther replied, 'If I have found favor in your sight, O king, and if it pleases the king, let my life be given me as my petition, and my people as my request'" (Esther 7:3).

Esther showed love, honor, and the utmost respect while addressing her husband. Doesn't your beloved deserve the same when you address serious or hurtful issues?

Remember the example of Queen Esther when attempting difficult discussions. Pray first. Display honor. Show respect. Love throughout.

Sometimes when you talk to God first, before going to your spouse with a concern or offense, you can work it out with you and God. Oftentimes, as for me, Mike has done nothing at all, and I'm the one who needs to make an adjustment. Always try to work it through first.

Any time you begin to feel discontentment looming in your heart, it's time for a discussion. But when you get to that point, always proceed like Queen Esther. Timing can be everything. And show love and respect in the process. Taking your spouse off your top ten favorite people list would not be advised.

## What do you do if you can't have a discussion with the person who has hurt you?

When we learn how to forgive difficult people, we become more like Jesus.

A very effective tool in releasing hurts and anger is writing the person a letter. One which you will never give to the "offender." The letter would only be for the purpose of you getting over the hurt and letting out your pent-up emotions.

Begin by writing all the things you want to say. The mean and nasty stuff. Then, move on to how they have hurt you. Next, write what you'd like to hear from them in response. After writing what you'd like to hear from this person, you'll most likely move on to understanding how they may have felt. Write whatever you want. You make the rules.

When you're done, delete. If handwritten, burn it or rip it up. The letter is for your eyes only. You don't want him/her to find it and be hurt; it's only for the purpose of you getting over your hurt.

Most of the time after doing this, you can release the person and clear out any bitterness in your heart. This can also be an exercise to prepare you for the upcoming conversation you'll have with the person. This formula can work with anyone. I've used it often and it always helps me. Writing a letter is a helpful tool to release any stored grudges.

I was able to share this tool with Brad. He later told me how, at first, writing out his feelings seemed odd. In spite of this, he decided to give it a try and began journaling his pent-up feelings. As he did this he was able to release most of the resentment he had built up toward his wife. When it came time for the consequent discussion, it was a much easier interaction.

## Let It Go

There was a time at church when a mom of a little girl in our children's ministry overreacted to something and unloaded all of her frustration out on me.

Her words were vicious and cutting, and to make matters worse, when I tried to talk in order to apologize, she put her hand in my face and proclaimed, "I'm not done!"

Finally, she paused, and I was able to apologize. You would have thought this would have calmed her down, but it didn't. She went right back into her unkind words directed right at me. Sadly, she ended up walking away angry.

The next week at church I looked up during worship,

and who do you think I saw on the worship team singing and raising her hand? Yes, *her*! The angry mom! Instead of worshipping, my mind raced to the week before. Focusing on God and praise became difficult for me. *How could she be on the worship team? I need to report her or something.* Funny how when we've been hurt, we turn into the spiritual police!

In the weeks to follow, every time I saw her onstage during church, worship became a challenge. I decided that every time I saw her, whether onstage or not, I would pray for her. It wasn't easy to do at first, but I stuck with it. Over time, noticing her singing or walking around church didn't spark negativity in me, and I grew to genuinely like her. Now I see her as another broken person, just like me, who needs healing and prayer.

I've overreacted to situations before and had to go back and apologize. We all have bad days.

### Don't Give Satan a Foothold

Allowing resentment to creep in will give Satan a foothold in your relationship, attacking the core of your vulnerability and trust. Resentment causes us to focus on *ME*. Satan wants you to focus on "me" and destroy "we." A lack of forgiveness will slowly erode trust and build resentment. A lack of trust will affect your sex life.

Gentlemen, do I have your attention now?

Trust is the foundation of a solid bond between husband and wife. If you don't forgive, it's hard to trust you. If you don't ask for forgiveness, why should anyone trust you?

When two forgivers come together, that's when the magic happens.

The Basics of Forgiveness:

*Accept God's forgiveness.*—Forgiveness begins with God. Accept Jesus Christ and be fully forgiven.

*Extend forgiveness to others.*—Don't hold on to offenses. Release anger and hurt.

*Ask for forgiveness.*—If you've been the offender, apologize and ask for forgiveness. And by the way, saying, "*If* I have done _____," or "*But* you did _____," is not asking for forgiveness. Adding "if" or "but" to an apology diminishes your appeal and oftentimes wipes it out. Instead say, "I'm sorry I have hurt you by [name the offense]. Please forgive me."

*Don't allow resentment to build up.*—At the first twinge of a grudge, address it. Don't ignore discontentment in your heart. Deal with it. Fast! There is something about talking about how we feel that allows us to let it go. Don't hold it in. Talk about your feelings in a kind and respectful manner. When angst builds up, we risk dumping on those we love the most as we relieve the pressure.

Have the difficult conversations. Talking through challenges—with love and respect—will enhance your relationship *and* your sex life.

## Do Whatever It Takes

Are you willing to do whatever it takes to keep your marriage free from resentment and bitterness? You can do it. You just need to decide you will always choose forgiveness. At the end of a long offense-filled day, forgiveness is a choice.

# Discussion Questions

- What does forgiveness look like to you?

- Do you ever confuse condoning an offense with forgiving an offense?

- Are you holding on to any bitterness in your heart?

- Do you believe forgiveness is a choice? Why or why not?

- Do you have any wounds from your past you need to find healing for? Consider talking to a pastor or counselor.

- Can you make a pact today to have a resentment-free marriage? Discuss why or why not.

- Is it hard for you to forgive?

- Did you grow up in a home filled with unconditional love and forgiveness? Discuss your feelings about your answer.

# Chapter Four
## Communication

Your marriage will rise and fall on communication. You can't have a great marriage without great communication. People in healthy, thriving marriages know how to express their feelings, wants, and needs, and know how to accept their partner's feelings, wants, and needs.

It sounds simple, doesn't it? Say what you want. Mean what you say. Listen. I wish it were that simple. But it simply is not. Not at all! In fact, healthy and clear verbal and nonverbal interaction will prove to be one of the most (if not *the most*) challenging hurdles in your marriage. But once you leap this hurdle, everything else will fall into place. The problem is, you will be leaping it as long as you are married.

We can know what healthy communication looks like and know what the right things to say are. We can have a plan for only using positive words and a resolution to only be constructive and continually build up the other person. We are determined to stick to our plan—and then something happens. A titanic obstacle gets in the way.

*Emotions.*

When our feelings get involved, we tend to send planning and logic sailing. Why? Because we feel hurt. We feel pain. We feel discounted. We feel betrayed. We feel unloved. We feel disrespected. We feel devalued. And the worst part about it is, it's coming from the person we think should love us the most. This makes it all the more difficult to sort out our feelings, wants, and needs.

Join me for an amusing tale titled, *The Josh and Shelly Saga*. Josh and Shelly are a young married couple, married for just over two years. They work in the same field but not for the same businesses. Josh and Shelly are wildly in love and enjoy many of the same activities. Both work full-time, with no student loans and no credit card debt. Life is good and financially free.

As Friday finally arrives and Josh finishes out his hard workweek, he daydreams often about his impending time with Shelly for the weekend. Shelly is over-the-top excited about closing out her workweek and spending Friday night and then two whole days with Josh. Shelly connects with Jessica who sits a few cubicles away.

"Hey, Jessica! You sure seemed focused today. I didn't even see you leave for lunch."

"Yeah, just making sure I get everything done by five today. Shelly, you did a fantastic job staying out of all the office drama this week! I wish I could navigate Claire the way you do."

"Oh, thank you! I've just been so busy, and plus I've had Josh on my mind. I can't wait to spend the weekend with him."

"Do you and Josh have any plans?"

"Hmm. Actually, no."

"Ah, too bad. Frank and I are headed to Palm Springs for

the weekend. I can't wait!"

"How fun! Enjoy your time. I'll see you on Monday."

"Yeah, see you Monday. I hope you enjoy your weekend with Josh."

"Thanks!"

Josh, being an introvert, avoids the office small talk and focuses on making a memorable impression with his boss. If Josh stays on track, he'll be next in line for a promotion. Knowing Shelly wants to get pregnant soon, Josh plans for their future. But for the time being, Josh plans his weekend in his head. Knowing a new Italian restaurant opened up in town, Josh wants to surprise Shelly by taking her there for dinner. He knows Italian is her favorite and made a reservation earlier in the week. Then Saturday morning Josh was hoping to cook breakfast for Shelly. Hanging around their house and doing fix-it projects recharges Josh. But more on his mind, he is hoping to get some "intimate" time with Shelly. Josh feels a bit disconnected from Shelly after spending the previous weekend with her family. A birthday and a wedding proved to be way too much "people time" for Josh. A weekend alone with Shelly has kept him thinking about her all day.

On her drive home, Shelly thinks about how fun it would be to spontaneously pack when she gets home and head to the beach for a weekend away with Josh. Inside she's feeling really jealous of her friend Jessica. Jessica and Frank take three times more trips than she and Josh do.

Shelly arrives home first and does a quick search on the Internet for bed-and-breakfast places by the beach. As Josh arrives home, so does a text on Shelly's phone. It's from Josh's best friend's wife, asking if they want to join them for dinner at a sushi restaurant. Shelly knows how much Josh enjoys his friend and wants to encourage the friendship.

"Josh, I got a text from Rebecca inviting us out for sushi tonight. Do you want to go?"

Knowing what an extrovert Shelly is, Josh figures Shelly really wanted to go.

"Sure. Let's go."

While Shelly texts Rebecca to confirm, Josh cancels the reservation he had made.

They join their friends for the evening, have an okay time, and arrive back home late. Exhausted from all the social interaction, Josh falls asleep quickly after getting into bed. Shelly can't sleep. Thinking about how fun a bed-and-breakfast would be, she wishes Josh were more spontaneous.

Feeling lonely and a bit frustrated with Josh, Shelly watches a late show and eats a bowl of popcorn followed by a bowl of ice cream.

In the morning, Josh gets up early and goes for a run. He returns home, showers, and gets dressed as quietly as possible so as not to wake Shelly, who is still sound asleep.

Josh goes into the kitchen and prepares coffee, french toast, eggs, and bacon. He cuts a single red rose from the bush in the backyard and puts it in some water and places it in the center of their kitchen table.

"Good morning," Shelly says cheerfully as she walks into the kitchen still not fully awake.

Josh is thinking how beautiful she looks even though

she's just gotten up. Her hair is messy, and she has her striped pajamas on, but she looks sexy to Josh.

"Good morning." Josh kisses her. He would love to pick her up and take her into the bedroom, but she doesn't seem interested. She just seems tired.

"Would you like some breakfast?"

*I shouldn't have eaten that ice cream last night.* "Just coffee, thanks."

"Okay."

Josh pours her some coffee. They sit at the kitchen table while he eats breakfast and she sips her coffee.

Josh's phone rings. He answers.

"Hi, Mom. What's up?"

Shelly feels really put out from the early morning call.

"Yes. . . Okay. . . I don't know, maybe? . . . Bye. Love you, too."

"What did your mom want?"

"She needs help rearranging her furniture today. Dad's back is out again."

"Sooooo. You going over there?"

"I don't know. Maybe."

"Well, just go."

"Hey, what's up with you?"

"You want to go, so just go."

"I didn't say I wanted to go."

"I can tell you want to go. You don't want to spend time with me."

"What? My parents need help. We always do what your parents want."

"Excuse me? What *my* parents want? When was the last time we did anything for my parents?"

"How about last weekend? We picked up the cake for your cousin's wedding, and we helped your mom clean up after the birthday party."

"Why are you being so mean? Okay, fine! We won't do anything for my family anymore!" Shelly begins to cry.

"Why are you crying?"

"Because you're so mean."

"Since I'm so mean, I'm going to go help my parents."

Josh grabs his keys and leaves.

Josh feels very alone, angry, and unappreciated.

Shelly feels devastated, pushed aside, and unloved.

Who's at fault?

Neither Josh nor Shelly intended to hurt the other; they both had good intentions. They both wanted to spend time together and desired to connect. And yet, they were both left feeling very alone and extremely undervalued. He didn't feel respected. She didn't feel cherished.

Let's rewind, shall we? And play this out in a more healthy and constructive manner.

...As Josh arrives home, a text comes in on Shelly's phone from friends inviting them out. After greeting each other, mixed with a few kisses, Josh says, "I love you."

"I love you, too."

Josh adds, "I couldn't wait to get home. I thought about you all day."

"I know. Me, too. I'm glad I get you to myself this weekend."

Josh relaxes by stripping down to his boxers and a T-shirt. Taking off his shoes, pants, and button-down shirt helps him to unwind. Shelly waits to tell Josh about the text invite until after he's settled in.

*Interlude: Ladies, most men need some time to wind down at the end of their workday. I give my husband time when he first gets home before I hit him with questions or engage in any serious conversation. Usually by the time he's done sorting through the mail, he's ready to talk. I sit back and wait. He lets me know when he's ready for interaction. Most women can shift gears fairly quickly and can't understand why a man needs this time. (Although, some women need this wind-down time as well.) Don't take offense at your man needing space when he first arrives home. You can be unwise about it and ignore this warning, but you'll most likely end up with a frustrated husband and be wondering why. Give him a little time. How much? If you can't seem to gauge it, just ask him. Have a discussion about it, and let him tell you. Learn about—know—each other, and do what works for you.*

Shelly and Josh engage in conversation about their day.

*Interlude: Men, your lady needs to talk with you. She wants to hear about your day and wants to share about*

*hers. Give her time. Listen. And don't try to fix any chal-*
*lenges she may bring up.*

Shelly tells Josh about the text she received. "Tom and Rebecca want us to join them for sushi tonight. I got a text from Rebecca when you got home. I let her know I'd talk with you about it."

Josh thinks for a minute. "How do you feel about going?"

"Well, I know how much you like to spend time with Tom. If you'd like to go, it would be okay with me."

Josh says, "I really wanted to spend time with just you this weekend. I feel a bit disconnected, and I'd love some downtime."

"I really wanted to be alone tonight as well. Should I tell her no?"

"Sounds good."

Shelly sends off a quick text. As she does that, Josh confirms their reservation on his phone.

Josh smiles and says, "How about some Italian tonight?"

"I love Italian food!"

"I know. I made a reservation at that new Italian restaurant. Do you want to go there?"

"How long do we have?"

"Long enough to *have some fun.* Do I need to woo you, or are you gonna give it up?"

They both erupt with laughter.

How could Shelly resist?

Fast-forward to the restaurant: As they wait for their

appetizers to arrive, Shelly thinks about Jessica.

"Jessica and Frank went to Palm Springs for the weekend," Shelly blurts out. "I feel a bit jealous. I'd love it if we could do more weekends away."

"Where would you want to go?"

"Well, I found this cute little bed-and-breakfast by the beach."

"How about we plan on going there next weekend? I feel tired and need a weekend home. The wedding and birthday last week were fun, but I'd really like to hang around the house this weekend."

"I understand. Thank you for going with me last week. It was sweet of you to help my mom. I know she really appreciated it."

"So what do you think?" Josh smiles as he looks into Shelly's eyes. "Can we hang at the house this weekend and go to the bed-and-breakfast next weekend?"

"Yes. Perfect."

Shelly feels loved and understood. "Josh, thank you for taking me to this restaurant. I love it!"

When they get home after dinner, they watch a movie together and share a bowl of popcorn. As they snuggle in bed, Shelly thinks, *My husband is so spontaneous. I'm the luckiest girl in the world.*

The next morning as Josh gets up, Shelly goes into the kitchen and makes some coffee.

Josh says, "I'm going for a run. How about I make us breakfast when I get back?"

"Sounds great. I really wanted to do some reading."

Josh goes for a run. When he gets back, he cuts a single rose from their yard, puts it in some water, and places it in the center of their table.

Heading for the shower, he asks, "Do you want to join me?" Shelly is happy to.

Later they sit at their kitchen table with the single red rose and eat the breakfast Josh prepared.

Josh's phone rings. He lets it go to voice mail, even though it's his mom.

Josh tells Shelly how beautiful she looks.

*Interlude: Men, we ladies never get tired of hearing how beautiful we are to you.*

Shelly thanks Josh for breakfast. After breakfast they clean the kitchen together. When they're almost done, Shelly says, "I'll finish up. Why don't you call your mom back and see what she wanted."

Josh dials his mom. "Hey Mom, what's up?" He walks out onto the patio while Shelly finishes up in the kitchen.

When Josh comes back in, he walks up behind Shelly, holds her around her waist, and begins kissing her on the neck.

"What did your mom want?"

"Apparently, my dad's back is out again and she needs help moving furniture."

"So, are we going over there?"

"I told her maybe we could come by after work Monday night. She said she'd make us dinner. I told her I'd check with you. What do you think?"

"Sounds great."

"Okay, I'll let her know."

"Hey, Josh, thank you."

"For what?"

"For dinner last night, for breakfast, and for taking me to the beach next week."

*Interlude: Ladies, men like to be thanked. It expresses how much you trust and appreciate him.*

The rest of the weekend was very restful and refreshing for both of them. And the following weekend they went to the lovely bed and-breakfast Shelly found. Everyone was happy and felt loved, valued, and appreciated.

## Healthy Communication

Begin by expressing love every day—verbal and nonverbal. Next, wrangle in your feelings. Filter every feeling through, *He/she loves me. He/she wants what's best for me. He/she would never want to hurt me.* This will give you a stronger *WE*, as well as a foundation of understanding and kindness. Any time your feelings don't line up with love and grace, go back to what you know is *true*. Settle in on this verse: "Finally, brethren, whatever is true, whatever is honorable, whatever is right, whatever is pure, whatever is lovely, whatever is of good repute, if there is any excellence and if anything worthy of praise, dwell on these things" (Philippians 4:8).

Dwell on what is true. *Believe* what is true. *He/she loves me. He/she wants what's best for me. He/she would never want to hurt me.* If negative thoughts about your spouse creep in, stop immediately. If you catch yourself chanting, *He doesn't care about me, She doesn't appreciate me,* know instantly you got it wrong and decide to view the situation correctly.

It doesn't matter what you *say*; what matters is what the other person *hears*. If your words cause a negative reaction, ask her what she heard. If your words cause him to withdraw, ask him what he heard. More than likely he/she didn't hear you correctly or you didn't communicate accurately. We don't receive information based on what we hear. We receive information based on *how it makes us feel.*

I was feeling needy and insecure. I asked Mike, "Do you love me?" I was hoping to hear, "I love you so much. In fact, I don't know what I'd do without you." Then the birds would start chirping and I'd dance around the kitchen with glee.

But that's not the response I got. Mike said, "I come home, don't I?"

Dagger!

*Of course you come home. This is where your dog is. And your garage and bed!*

I walked away wounded and angry by the perceived spear through my tender heart. And said nothing.

Weeks went by with the dagger firmly rooted. Finally—gathering all the courage I could muster up—abashedly broaching the love subject once again, I regurgitated what I heard him say.

Mike confirmed I had heard him correctly: "I come home, don't I?" *Yeah, I got that part, thank you.*

This time he continued, "I love coming home. I love coming home *to you.* There are lots of other things I could do, but I always want to come home."

*Ohhhhhh! This was a compliment.*

I had allowed a compliment to wound and torment me for weeks! And all because I didn't stop and ask him to explain.

Ask. Don't assume the worst.

Getting in touch with your feelings and learning how to fully communicate wounds, wishes, and desires will be a critical factor in your marriage. When conversations begin to get heated, ask yourself, "How am I feeling?" And then express your feelings. Feelings begin with "I" statements, not "you" statements.

Healthy:
- I feel discounted right now.
- I feel hurt about what I just heard.
- I feel like I am disappointing you, and I feel sad about that.
- I feel unloved when I hear those words.
- I'm confused, and I don't understand.

Unhealthy and destructive:
- You made me mad.
- You hurt me by saying you don't want to go with me.

- When you didn't call, you basically said you didn't care.
- You don't care about my feelings.
- You're being mean.
- You're acting like a selfish [you fill in the blank].

When we start with "you" it immediately puts the other person on the defensive. When you express how you are feeling, this will make it easier for the other to digest what you're saying.

Ladies, cover your eyes for a bit; I'd like to tell the men something. Men, do you want her to hear you when it comes to what you want and need? Talk like this: "I feel [fill in the blank], or I'm feeling [fill in the blank], and what I really need from you is [fill in the blank]." Now you're speaking our language and we'll get you. If my husband ever says, "I feel...and I need you to...," he's got me completely—ready and willing—to do whatever he needs. Most women will *feel* the same.

Hello again, ladies...

In their book, *Love & War*, John and Stasi Eldredge explain inner struggles we all face as men and women. John notes that real and authentic strength for a man is not about the size of his muscles; but instead, what matters is a man's "*inner* strength." When men use their God-given strength in destructive ways, it's most commonly either by becoming "passive and silent, or domineering and violent." Either choice can be very harmful for a relationship. Stasi points out that when women use their God-given "tenderness and vulnerability" in destructive ways, they "either become controlling or desperately needy." Women may either withhold vulnerability or look to their husband to fill all of their needs. Either choice can be utterly destructive for a marriage. Moreover, Stasi adds that her weight was a way she kept control of her world and a way to shield herself from intimacy.[1]

Oftentimes when a man gets angry it's because he can't express his feelings and reverts to anger. Some men just withdraw. If you're in a discussion with your man and he seems to be getting fired up, try asking: "Are you feeling disrespected right now?" "Discounted?" "Unappreciated?" "Did I hurt you?" And then listen to what he has to say without interrupting him. Give him time to express his feelings. (This works for both men and women.)

Ladies, if he becomes angry and you begin to feel scared, communicate this right away. Let him know how you're feeling, and ask him to lower his intensity.

Many times what we women do is begin to cry when tension arises. This can be grossly unfair if used in a manipulative way. Crying causes him to feel powerless. This is not to say that you should hold back tears if you need to cry. All I am saying is, don't use tears as a way to manipulate. This will not get you any closer to a healthy resolution.

What's best is open communication where both parties can express their desires, hurts, and needs. Don't allow tears to shut down the communication process.

Another tactic we women use is the "You're being mean"

---

1 John and Stasi Eldredge, *Love & War* (Colorado Springs, CO: WaterBrook Publishing, 2011), 48.

card. We pull it out like the ace of spades. I've done it. And it really isn't fair. Seriously, what can he say to that? It's not helpful. Be specific about what's causing your sorrow and pain.

For instance:

*I felt demeaned when I heard. . .*

*I felt abandoned when. . .*

*I feel misunderstood and tossed aside by. . .*

These types of statements will be hugely more productive than "You're being mean." At least he has something to work with, and the issue can be resolved.

Keep the lines of communication open. Stray away from anything that shuts down healthy interaction. Healthy communication—even after multiple decades of marriage—still remains as one of the biggest challenges for my husband and me. We continually strive to resolve disagreements, share information, and petition the other for wants and needs in a way that strengthens and doesn't destroy. Your interaction can either strengthen or break down your union. Keep working at it, and never let up. Never give up on pushing aside *ME* for a better *WE*.

## Be Clear

Clear communication begs a response. Any time there can be any question, or when critical facts are necessary, always ask the other person to repeat back to you what he/she heard. Especially if your beloved seems affected negatively by what was said.

Always repeat information.

Receive the information. Repeat what you heard. And then respond. Sometimes the healthiest response is sharing how you *feel* about what your spouse said. If misinterpretation or misunderstandings arise, you can hold up a stop sign and start over. Many arguments can be prevented with this method.

Let's look at how *potential* arguments can be avoided with clear, healthy communication:

Josh arrives home and announces, "Let's go out for dinner tonight. I'm sick of eating in."

Shelly feels hurt by this. "Josh, I thought you liked my cooking. I feel really hurt."

Josh: "No, I love your cooking. I wanted to take you out because you've been working so hard, and tonight I would like your full attention and no dishes to clean."

During the day, Josh lets Shelly know he needs some "adult time."

They both arrive home from a hard day, totally exhausted. Shelly falls asleep early. In the morning Shelly rises early, and Josh finds her scrubbing the kitchen floor. Josh thinks Shelly is avoiding him.

"Shelly, are you trying to avoid me?"

"No, not at all! I dropped syrup on the floor while making breakfast for you. Go back to our room, and in five minutes I'll have breakfast in bed for you. And it will include *dessert*."

Both of these scenarios could have ended in fights with fallout damage to their relationship, if either Josh or Shelly had not been vulnerable in trusting the other with their feelings.

## Trust/Sex/Talking

The average man has a difficult time expressing how important sex is to him.

Men, I'm going to help you out with this. To be more specific, comedian Steve Harvey will help you out with this.

Steve Harvey was on the *Tonight Show* in 2015.

While he was being interviewed, he said, "Women don't know how important sex is to a guy. You can't overstate this enough. It's everything to us. It's the reason we go to college. I went to college because I heard you could have sex when you got there. It's the reason that men bathe. If there were no women, we wouldn't even bathe!"

Very funny interview.

Very compelling information.

As important as this need is for a man, many struggle to communicate this persistent desire with their wives.

Why?

Perhaps he's afraid of rejection. Maybe he fears he will be laughed at, humiliated even. Asking his wife for sex can be a very scary and vulnerable time for a man.

And so he remains quiet.

I'm going to help the ladies out with voicing a deep desire most women have. Most? It's probably *all*.

Men, your wife has a need to connect through conversation. She needs to be heard. She needs to be understood. She connects and feels valued through conversation.

Ladies, the need you feel in wanting to connect with your man is the same need he feels in wanting to connect with you through sex.

When he approaches you for "fun," realize he not only wants sex; he wants to *connect with you*. Much like your need to connect through conversation. Imagine if he stopped talking to you for days. How would you feel? You know where I'm going with this.

Don't stop *connecting* as a couple, verbally and, well—two thumbs up—*physically*.

Here's the formula for over-the-top communication and connection. Talk every day. Listen. Interact with your beloved. And have sex often.

Ladies, when he feels the need to connect and express his love physically, don't dismiss this request lightly. *WHAT?!* I can hear some of you ladies screaming, "*Don't I have a say in this?*" Yes, of course you do. But always ask yourself, "Would I want him to stop talking to me?" At the very least, make an appointment for a later time.

Let me give you a little hint. The more you say yes, the more he'll feel connected to you and the more he will talk to you. It's a very happy formula for everyone.

# Discussion Questions

- Ladies, how do you feel about the idea of giving him space when he first arrives home? Men, do you feel you need this time? Why or why not?

- If your spouse turned you down for sex, how would you feel? Discuss how you would resolve this tension as a couple.

- Did you grow up in a home where it was easy or difficult to share your needs and desires? How do you think this will affect you as a couple?

- Do you have any fears attached to getting married? Share them.

- What are you most excited about as you begin your life as a married couple?

- What do you think will be your biggest obstacles in communicating fully with each other?

- What issues do you think would be hardest to discuss?

- Would you be willing to reach out to a professional, as in, a pastor or therapist, if you needed help to overcome barriers in your marriage?

# Chapter Five
## Unpacking Your Baggage

When my husband and I glided into married life, we both arrived with a lot of emotional baggage. And we've been unpacking ever since. Our bags were large and fierce. We would unload as much as we could on the other person. Slowly we learned how to unpack and unload our extra baggage in a healthy way.

We all have baggage from our past. Some more than others. It's dangerous to assume you're not bringing baggage into your marriage. Have you ever had your heart broken? Did you have an ongoing childhood illness? Maybe you were teased or bullied as a kid, or your parents divorced. Maybe you've been through a divorce yourself. Or struggled with pornography or same-sex attraction. These will bring along issues that need to be worked through.

Perhaps you've got more serious scars, such as sexual abuse, physical abuse, serious childhood trauma, or emotional abuse. Anything from your past that caused harm will be carried into marriage.

We think we can bury our hurts and not acknowledge them. Then, when least expected, buried pain will bubble up to the surface and spill over as guilt, shame, rage, insomnia, panic attacks, depression, addictions, eating disorders, and the list can go on and on.

But don't despair; as I said at the start of this chapter, my husband and I had our own baggage to work through, and at the other side of struggle emerged a stronger, healthier *WE*. We tackled, and continue to tackle, our difficulties *together*.

If your spouse has a problem or struggle, *your marriage* has a struggle. You can't point a finger; it falls on both of you. It's not *YOU* have a challenge. It's *WE* have a challenge. In marriage all problems are a *WE* problem, not a *YOU* problem. In Ecclesiastes 4:12 it says, "And if one can overpower him who is alone, two can resist him. A cord of three strands is not quickly torn apart."

A united, cemented fortress of a strong marriage will prove to be a powerful tool for God. One He will use in mighty ways. All the pain, anguish, and turmoil from your past, God will use in beautiful ways if you allow Him to. Struggles can bloom as blessings. Our biggest weaknesses can transform into our strongest strengths.

When you take the first step of recognizing hurts—bring each to the forefront—and then unpack each hurt together, they will no longer have power over you.

Secrets have power.

When Mike and I got married, I had a huge secret. No one knew about it. I held my secret close and tight. Within the first year of our marriage, Mike discovered what I had been hiding since I was sixteen years old.

I had an eating disorder.

Dealing with it and hiding it—all on my own—had

become commonplace for me. This beast ruled me and kept me powerless. And then, suddenly, I wasn't alone anymore; Mike jumped into the pit with me. He jumped full bore, and roaring like a lion! My secret predicament became a *WE* predicament. But neither of us knew how to deal with such a beast as an eating disorder.

You need to understand this was back in the early '80s, a time when model Lesley Lawson, better known as Twiggy, was the icon for women as the ideal body shape. Little was known about eating disorders then. In 1983 Karen Carpenter, a famous singer, died from heart failure due to an eating disorder, and it was then the disease became more public and talked about.

We had no idea what to do. I thought I was fine, but he was scared stiff.

I recall him shrieking, "You could die! You have to stop this!"

His next step was to tell everyone who cared about us. He told my parents, his parents, family, and friends about my "secret" struggle.

My stealthy life was over.

You would have thought I'd have been mad at him, but I wasn't. Not at all. I knew he was just scared and that he loved me. He didn't know what to do, and he was calling in all the help he could reach for. It was probably one of the greatest expressions of love anyone has ever shown me.

And it probably saved my life.

Out of all the people he told, one person knew what I needed to do. Judy (her real name), a childhood friend who was a bridesmaid at my wedding, called me practically every day. She'd say, "Lu, you have to get help." It was always the same message. Over. And. Over. She'd call and say the same thing, "Lu, you need to get help." It was truth mixed with love.

Finally, I reached out and called a therapist who specialized in eating disorders. It was the first step to my recovery. I stayed in therapy for two years. At the end of those two years, I became a Christian—a full-fledged follower of Jesus Christ.

God has used my story to help so many others, and today I wear it like a medal of honor. It was a battle Mike and I tackled together and overcame. It made *ME* stronger, and it made *WE* stronger.

Today in our marriage, we have no secrets. As issues arise from our past, we bring each one to the table, and we devour them—together. Soldiers in battle bond together. When you battle issues as a couple, it will bond you like superglue.

In marriage you need to learn how to use brokenness to draw you closer. One way to do this is to unpack baggage as a team.

Now, let's dig in.

## Past Relationships

Most likely, you've had other boyfriends or girlfriends before you got together. Almost everyone has had a broken heart at one time or another. If you haven't been in a previous relationship, this would be an issue to unpack with all the feelings related to never having been in a relationship. More common, however, are the dating disasters gone wrong, which left you damaged and limping. Either of these scenarios could have left you with feelings of rejection and despair.

If you grew up in the church, you've heard "stay pure until your wedding day." Well, now you fully know why. Everything from your past is brought with you into your marriage. You are taking every kiss, every touch, every crush with you. I'd be stupid to think none of you have been sexually active. You may have even experimented with the same sex.

Please do not carry any guilt or shame with you. God created us as sexual beings. He designed us for intimate contact. Don't beat yourself up over this; just make things right today. If you've messed up in this area, you can still start over.

Maybe you've gone too far as a couple. Every day is a day to start new with God and do relationship His way. Make amends with God, ask for forgiveness, apologize to each other, and move on. Decide you will hold off until after your wedding. You'll be glad you did.

Trust and vulnerability will be critical foundations of your marriage. Trust your partner with your past. Talk about past relationships. Do not go into detail about every little thing, especially every *physical* thing. Be general. Talk through mistakes, heartbreaks, and regrets. This will be a lesson on trust. Be understanding and forgiving.

Treat each other the way God treats us. With love and unconditional acceptance.

## Pornography

We have all been affected by pornography. In our culture today, it is unavoidable. Some have been more affected than others.

During premarital counseling, Troy talked through his previous problem with pornography with their pastor and Sarah, his bride-to-be. This information was not uncommon for the pastor to hear about. Now, with his wedding day approaching, Troy had tremendous guilt associated with his past behavior. Sarah was extremely considerate and accepting, and with the help of their pastor, they were able to talk through Troy's feelings. Because Troy talked about it and because Sarah didn't hold it against him, they were able to not allow Troy's past to be a barrier to their intimacy.

Talking through this issue made them stronger, and years later their marriage is thriving.

When we create a safe environment to talk about tough issues, and we accept each other's downfalls, we breed a culture of victory over struggles.

Ladies, if pornography has a grip on your man or if it did in the past, be a safe place for him to talk about it. This will help him to overcome. If you have any uneasiness—concerned you will not be able to live up to images he's seen—talk about your feelings.

Pornography can be a struggle for women, too. Maybe not as common, but the same applies for both men and women.

## Sexual and Physical Abuse

Author Dorie VanStone overcame sexual and physical abuse and writes she "felt dirty, ashamed, and unworthy of human love," along with feelings that somehow others could see she felt different on the inside, even when she tried to emulate others on the outside. Dorie states, "And I thought that everyone else could see inside me." If you are a victim, you can most likely relate to this.[1]

The first step in dealing with sexual abuse is to acknowledge it. A victim needs to come to terms with the reality of their past. Talking about what happened enables one to release repressed pain, and shame. Know that many people (I consider myself in this group) have had victory and rise above sexual abuse. If this is part of your story, *you can, too.*

Steven and Veronica were planning on getting married. They made an appointment to talk with me. Veronica had been molested as a child and had suffered horrendous acts, and then subsequent acting out had occurred due to the abuse. (Please understand acting out is not uncommon with victims of sexual abuse.) She and Steven feared how this would play out in their marriage.

After they were married, I checked back with Steven and Veronica and received an e-mail from her. I'm sharing this with permission. "Meeting with you was a pivotal moment in our relationship. Prior to our time together, Steven actually struggled with seeing a future with me because of my past. It was hard for him to deal with, that my history was so extensive. But after talking with you he realized the truth in

---

1 Dorie N. VanStone and Erwin W. Lutzer, *No Place to Cry: The Hurt and Healing of Sexual Abuse* (Chicago, IL: Moody Publishers, 1992), 15–16.

what you told me. . . . 'How would you have picked anything different when you didn't know that different existed?' When this was revealed to him, Steven finally felt peace and was able to move forward."

They began their marriage with honesty, vulnerability, sensitivity, and trust, which laid the foundation for many happy years together. This is an excellent example of grappling with one's past in order to make *WE* stronger.

If physical or sexual abuse is in your past, I want you to know *it is not your fault!* Many people who have been victims feel like somehow they were at fault. God has placed in every child's heart a natural desire to love and respect his or her parents, explain authors Dorie VanStone and Erwin W. Lutzer in their book, *No Place to Cry: The Hurt and Healing of Sexual Abuse*. For an innocent and trusting child, the idea that Mommy or Daddy could intentionally hurt me, or abandon me, is unfathomable, and therefore, the child concludes that he or she somehow deserves the abuse. And if that weren't enough, the child also assumes responsibility of said abuse, determines he or she is "awful," and feels a tremendous amount of guilt. This becomes an overwhelming burden for a child.[2]

As children, when our environment becomes unbearable we find coping mechanisms to navigate the world around us. Volumes can be said about sexual abuse and overcoming it. What I'd like to emphasize is, *don't hide your pain, and don't allow it to be a barrier in your marriage.* Begin your healing

---

2 Ibid., 58.

by letting out your pain, either by talking or journaling. If you can't seem to put it into words, then write it out. Even after ten years of marriage, Stephanie, a dear friend, was still unable to speak about what had happened to her as a child. She wrote her story out and then gave it to her husband to read. He lovingly embraced her past. This was the beginning of her healing.

Holding it in only gives the abuse power; releasing it gives the power back to you.

Dr. Dan B. Allender reports that one of the biggest lies victims tell themselves is that everything is fine—ignoring emotional wounds. The first step is to face whatever abuse was endured and to fully acknowledge what happened. Then one can begin the work of restoration. [3]

Don't allow the pain of your past to define your future.

I met Richard, a volunteer on our church security team, when he was assigned to my son-in-law who was preaching for the weekend services. Being at a megachurch, pastor security detail is taken very seriously. At the close of the Saturday night services, Kyle, my son-in-law, told Richard, "Thank you, sir! You can go now. I'm good."

What Richard said impressed me greatly. "I'm not going anywhere until you are in your car."

Let me tell you, Richard is not someone you'd want to mess with. His physique and demeanor command any room. While his dedication exemplifies faithful service and his physical structure is considered very intimidating, the most

---

3 Dr. Dan B. Allender, *The Wounded Heart: Hope for Adult Victims of Childhood Sexual Abuse* (Colorado Springs, CO: NavPress, 2008), 14.

impressive quality about Richard is his tender heart. He has a love for people and for the Lord.

When Richard isn't volunteering at church, he works as a SWAT police officer. While talking with him one day, he shared how his mom and dad had physically abused him. It grieved me to hear him talk of the beatings he had endured as a child.

"It's an ongoing process," he said when I asked how he deals with his past. "I make the choice to forgive each day."

He went on to say he was divorced. "In my first marriage I cheated on my wife and didn't talk about my past. I tried to reconcile with her, but it was too late. We were both broken, and we didn't know how to be broken together. In my marriage now, I talk about my past and I communicate how I'm feeling. You can't keep silent about the hurts from your past; it will come out in destructive ways."

Richard now has a beautiful family, walks faithfully with the Lord, and has a godly wife who loves him deeply. God restored his life.

God can restore your hurt, too, if you have physical abuse in your past. Don't ignore it. Don't kid yourself that it will just go away. You've got to face your past, work through it (either by talking about it and/or talking with a trained professional), and then look to your future.

## Emotional Abuse
- "You're no good."
- "I hate you."
- "You're worthless."

- "I wish you were never born."

You may have heard statements like these from the mouths of those who were supposed to love and protect you. Some of you were rejected, abandoned even. You may feel unlovable and fear abandonment. This will come out in your marriage.

You may even be playing negative statements in your head and repeating them to yourself when the circumstances of life don't go your way.

Even after many years of marriage, Fred fears Gail will leave him when they have disagreements, especially when Gail's feelings have been hurt. Gail struggles to completely understand this. It just doesn't make sense to her, but feelings don't often make sense. When Fred begins to feel he will be abandoned, he shares his insecurities with Gail, and she reassures him of her love. They both know this stems from emotional abuse from Fred's childhood, and instead of allowing his past to destroy their future, they face it and address the issue. This could be an avenue that pulls them apart, but they use it to build a stronger marriage by being open and vulnerable with each other.

While under pressure, Larry, a highly successful man, will repeat awful phrases in his mind that his mother frequently launched at him. "You're never going to amount to anything" will begin to play in his head. On days the recording starts playing, he'll talk with his wife and she'll remind him who he is, how much he's loved, and how he belongs to God. This type of vulnerable communication will not only help you work through such struggles; it also enables your spouse to help by being more sensitive.

## Trying to Hide Struggle

God did not create us to combat struggles on our own—we are to love and to be loved.

*Healthy* relationships give abuse victims the power to heal and overcome abuse. Sadly, many lack the ability to trust and therefore isolate themselves.

Relationships of those who have been abused can be more difficult because abuse creates shame and mistrust and can limit emotional vulnerability. *Healthy* relationships have healing power "to nurture the soul and heal the wounds of abuse."[4]

The work to create healthy relationships takes courage, trust, and time. Be willing to take the baby steps and strides toward healing *together*. When we hide inner battles from our spouse, they can inadvertently kick us where it hurts. If you poke someone in the side, it may tickle and you'll hear a chuckle. But if that same person has a stomachache or injury and you poke, you'll get a growl. This is what happens in many marriages. We fail to let our loved one know where it hurts, and then innocently, he/she may say or do something that peels open a wound. All-out combat can ensue. Our sweetheart becomes the enemy.

When we fail to communicate where it hurts, our partner doesn't know not to poke us there.

---

4 Steven R. Tracy, *Mending the Soul: Understanding and Healing Abuse* (Grand Rapids, MI: Zondervan Publishing, 2008), 125.

Ladies, if he forgets to call one day and it destroys you—guess what? It's not about the missed call. There is something deeper going on, and you need to address whatever past hurt is causing you to overreact to a forgotten phone call.

Gentlemen, if she prepares dinner for you and she's running behind, and then you don't like what she made and this causes you to become enraged because you feel she doesn't care about you—guess what? It wasn't about the dinner.

Any time your reaction to anything is greater than the perceived offense, that's a clue you've got something from your past to discuss and unpack. Things can happen—triggers—causing hurts from our past to pop up. Look for triggers and deal with them. Ignoring these will not make them go away.

Part of unpacking our baggage is talking through our hurts and issues.

You may need to get healing before you join your life with another. You may be thinking, *When I get married, then I'll feel whole and not broken anymore.* This is not going to happen. If you feel broken now, you will feel broken married, too. You cannot look to another person to heal your pain. You'll just be married *and* in pain. And while loving each other can help toward healing, expecting another person to be your solution to unresolved pain will set you up for colossal disappointment. Many marriages have split over unresolved pain and trauma that seeped out and exploded—consequently destroying the marriage and family.

There seems to be a stigma around reaching out for therapy. We may fear what people think. Better to get help than to have a terrible life and a failing marriage. When I've counseled people to seek professional help, I've often heard, "But I can't afford it." If you need it, you can't afford not to. A destroyed life, a destroyed marriage, a destroyed family is *way* more expensive than therapy.

Look to your future and give your marriage the best start possible. I know we've discussed some pretty heavy issues, and I pray none of these apply to you—but if they do, better to expose it now before it can damage your marriage. And please know with certainty there is nothing in your past God can't heal you from today.

Dr. Dan B. Allender asserts that the essence of biblical trust is relying on God for the preservation of our souls. When we belong to God, no one can shame, disgrace, or possess our souls. No matter what has been done to us—our bodies or otherwise—our eternal security rests in God alone.[5]

In this we can completely and eternally trust, my friends.

---

5 Allender, *The Wounded Heart*, 71.

# Discussion Questions

- Do you have any unresolved hurts and pain from your past?

- Did you grow up in a home where you could talk about your feelings?

- Have you or anyone in your family ever reached out for professional help or attended an overcomers group like Alcoholics Anonymous?

- Pick an issue from your past and unpack it together. Take turns being the one sharing and the one listening.

- How do you feel about seeking out professional help if necessary?

# Chapter Six
## Your Feelings Lie

It was a beautiful day in Southern California, and I was feeling particularly grateful. As a gift, my brother and sister-in-law arranged my flight to visit them in New Jersey. Everything had been taken care of except my seat assignment. My husband was happy to help with this last detail and opened his laptop. To my dismay the only seats left were in the back and in the middle, right smack between two other passengers. There was, however, a window seat toward the front of the plane, but the seat was an extra fifty dollars.

Mike asked me if I wanted to purchase the window seat. It seemed unappreciative and greedy to spend the extra money when there was a seat assignment for no extra charge.

"No," was my response.

"Okay," Mike said and clicked the middle seat in the back.

I went back to working on the laundry. (Marriage isn't always fun and games—sometimes it's dirty dishes, cleaning toilets, organizing family events, and loads of laundry.) As I worked on the laundry I started thinking about my middle seat on the plane, *for a five-hour flight!* I created a picture of my five-hour ordeal. There I would be, shoehorned in with Attila the Hun asleep on my shoulder and Chewbacca breathing on me on the other side. The more I thought about it, the more increasingly agitated and unhappy I became. I did try and stop my racing, distressed thoughts by telling myself, *You should be happy! You're going to see your brother and sister-in-law! Knock it off!*

That worked for about thirty seconds, and I went right back to my party with Chewbacca. Going into the kitchen to heat up my coffee, I gave words to my thoughts and announced to Mike, "All of my peace, joy, and happiness are gone." (Now, keep in mind, my flight wasn't until another four days. I had allowed my thoughts to ruin a perfectly great day.) As I grabbed my coffee from the microwave—hoping it would help to self-soothe my suffering—I decided to send a plea up to God. *God, please, if there is any way, please change my seat*, and I slammed the microwave shut.

My plight *felt* hopeless.

"I paid the fifty bucks and got you the window seat. . . ." Those glorious words danced out of my husband's mouth— and I'm certain I heard the Amen Choir singing, "Hallelujah," too!

Instantly, I began to sob. Not cute little sobs, mind you, gut-wrenching sobs.

Flinging my arms around Mike, a "Honey, thank you!" managed to emerge among the tears.

I was so incredibly thankful, immediately switching to thoughts of my wonderful, kind, and loving husband. In fact, I thought about what a wonderful husband I had all day. Instead of focusing on all the good in my life, I became immersed in a sea of negative thinking and made the choice to focus on what I was sure would be a horrible flight *four days away*.

I could have focused on Mike helping me to get my seat. *And be thankful*. I could have focused on my brother's kindness in paying for my flight. *And be thankful*. I could have focused on the great day I was having. *And be thankful*. But I didn't do that. I focused—hyperfocused—on a future "disaster" that never happened.

## Consumed with ME

My feelings had convinced me my seat issue was what was most important. My feelings were telling me my life was horrible and there was no reason for peace, joy, or happiness. I had allowed this somewhat ridiculous problem to turn into a big hullabaloo. At the core of this was selfishness. I was consumed with *ME*. Allowing a pattern of focusing in on *ME*, and negative thoughts, will hurt *WE*. Too much thinking about *ME* and trying to make *ME* happy can destroy *WE*. Plus, it doesn't honor God. "Now we who are strong ought to bear the weaknesses of those without strength and not just please ourselves. Each of us is to please his neighbor for his good, to his edification" (Romans 15:1–2).

Lucky for me, Mike decided to ride in on a white horse and be my hero. He displayed other-centeredness. Maybe he put himself in my position and thought, *I wouldn't want to sit in between Chewbacca and Attila the Hun*, and decided to *save me*. Actually, Mike does this kind of thing often (Men, take note!). He lets me know how valuable I am with his actions, intentionally looking for ways to bless me. This makes us stronger as a couple.

My husband "rescues" me often. Ladies, be willing to let your man sweep you up and rescue you. He wants to. Most men love rescuing a "damsel in distress." Let him open the jam jar for you, solve your dilemma, and show off his muscles—let him save the day!

We can always find something to be upset about. We find what we look for. I'm going to repeat this: *We find what we look for.* Stop and think about this for a second. When we look for good we find it. When we look for bad we find it. Train yourself to focus on the good in every circumstance. Train yourself to look for the good in your spouse. Train yourself to focus on what's beautiful and noble about him/her.

It's imperative that we harness our thoughts: "We are destroying speculations and every lofty thing raised up against the knowledge of God, and we are taking every thought captive to the obedience of Christ" (2 Corinthians 10:5).

You can do this. We can do this! We can take our thoughts captive, especially in marriage, and use them to regulate our feelings. Feelings are powerful. Unfortunately, they can lie to us, too. Which is why you also need to control your actions regardless of how you feel.

What does this look like?

## Taking Thoughts Captive

Begin each day with thankfulness. Remind yourself daily of the many blessings you have, "always giving thanks for all things in the name of our Lord Jesus Christ" (Ephesians 5:20). If you just slept in a bed, thank God for it! *Thank You, God, for my wonderful wife/husband. Thank You, God, for a hot shower. Thank You, God, for clothes. Thank You, God, for [you fill in the blank] today.*

I was once behind an elderly gentleman in line at the grocery store. The clerk asked him how he was. "When I woke up this morning," he said with a big smile, "I had a pulse; everything was up from there!"

Sometimes we neglect to be thankful for the most basic necessities. The extraordinary becomes ordinary. Think about the miracle of sight. We expect to be able to see, but for some, this would be a miracle. Think about life before you met your special someone. You've probably spent much of your life wondering if you'd ever meet what some like to call "the one," and now you've found him/her. Be thankful for him every day. Never take her for granted; be grateful for her love each day.

You are probably thinking, *Of course, that's easy to do!*

Okay, sure. You are thinking that *now*, but talk to me after you find out he snores really loudly and you're having trouble sleeping. Or when he has another softball tournament and will be gone *another* night after your mom invited you both to a family birthday party on that day. Or when he forgets to pay the electric bill and your power just got turned off. Or when he comes home spent because of a big project he's working on at work and doesn't want to talk with you. Or when he leaves his dirty dishes in the sink and his dirty socks around the house.

Talk to me when she locks her keys in the trunk of her car *again* and you have to drive an hour to go help her. Or when she's crying over the jeans she can't fit into and you have no idea how to console her. Or when she's telling you how to drive. Or when she makes you late for church because her hair wasn't just right. Or when she makes you late for your friend's wedding because "she has nothing to wear." Or when she has you drive to three different stores looking for the lipstick she saw on the morning show. Or when you've waited all day to "be intimate" and she falls asleep because she went into work early after staying up late the night before baking cupcakes for a friend's shower.

Not to mention the things that will just plain irritate you about him/her. The way he answers the phone. The way she chews her gum. His sneeze. Her snorts. The way he blows his nose. The way she laughs at you when you trip or bang your head.

Talk to me then. What do you do with these challenges?

When he snores, you thank God for a man in your bed and use your time awake for prayer. Be thankful for a man who is strong and can play softball, for a man who pays the bills *usually* and for the chance to enjoy a candlelight dinner, for a man who works hard, for a man who has arms to hold you and feet to play footsie with and a nose that can smell your perfume.

Men, when she's stuck, thank God for a woman who calls you to rescue her, and not some other guy. Thank God for a woman with feelings, not a Stepford wife. Be thankful for a wife who cares about your safety, cares how she looks, cares and loves you and others, is beautiful, and all the while, possesses a good sense of humor.

Keep this verse "flying" around in your head: "In everything give thanks; for this is God's will for you in Christ Jesus" (1 Thessalonians 5:18).

You will most likely encounter much greater challenges than an unfavorable seat assignment in your future as husband and wife. It's important to keep each other grounded on the truths of God's Word and focus on surrendering your life to God and each other *daily*.

Consider what my dear friend and fellow pastor's wife told me:

> *I believe that one of the biggest lies is that ANY circumstance or situation will ever bring true security and peace. Standing with hands open to God—surrendering expectations, surrendering perceived needs, allowing Him to be our one and only source of dependence, is the best safeguard against the barrage of lies. This is what the world and Satan would have us believe about contentment. Our feelings/emotions are how Satan often gets a foothold.*
> —RENEE RUTHERFORD

## Let God Fill Your Gaps

When we go to God for our needs, security, and peace, He will fill us to the point of overflow. Expecting a spouse to satisfy all of our desires and needs will create a huge gap in our marriage. No one person can fulfill all of your wants and needs. It's a surefire road to discontentment. If you are looking to marriage to bring missing peace, happiness, and contentment, all you'll be left with is an even greater gap between you and your expectations. On the other hand, when we are thankful for every kind gesture and thoughtful word, we will soon find our hearts overflowing with love and gratefulness.

Marriage will not make you whole. A thriving marriage is when two *whole* people come together and choose to love each other unconditionally—faults, failures, and all. Two empty, needy people coming together—looking to the other to have their needs met—produces an empty, needy marriage. Wholeness comes when God supplies contentment, and from this supply we unselfishly give, putting the other person first: "And my God will supply all your needs according to His riches in glory in Christ Jesus" (Philippians 4:19).

When feelings lie and tell us we are not receiving all "we should" from our spouse, discontentment grows. Arguments become about trying to get what we want from the other. We have expectations, and when our spouse fails to meet our expectations, we feel hurt and lash out.

Warren W. Wiersbe tells a story about an elderly man who asked if Dr. Wiersbe would perform a wedding for him and his soon-to-be bride. Not in the habit of performing weddings for strangers, Dr. Wiersbe asked that he bring in the bride-to-be so they could all talk. This gentleman agreed, but before doing so, he wanted to explain a few things. Both he and *his lady* had been married before. . .to each other! Anger, pride, and bitterness had separated them over thirty years prior. They got into a fight and separated. Pride prevented apologies. They made the mistake of divorcing and living alone *for over thirty years!* This couple, who still loved each other—*after thirty years*—had allowed bitterness, anger, and pride to steal the joy they could have had together. After all that time, they finally realized how foolish they had been and were hoping the Lord would give them happiness together for however many years they had left. Bitterness and anger are deadly.[1]

It's never too late to turn from bitterness, anger, and pride. Could you imagine allowing an argument to spiral to the point of leaving each other for thirty years? I guarantee both parties were trying to get *what they wanted, what they deserved, what they needed*, from the other. In the end they both ended up lonely, empty, and alone. That's what happens when we demand to have what we expect we *deserve* from another—we usually end up with nothing or close to it. It's like capturing someone and then demanding they love you. Hollow. Dead. Void. Meaningless.

Feelings can tell you he doesn't love you when he has to work late, when he spends hours on a memory game trying to name all the Pokémon characters, or when he forgets to pick up your allergy medication. Feelings can tell you she doesn't love you when she seems blasé about sex, when she forgets you hate salmon and makes it for dinner, or when she's on the phone with her mom but you had plans to watch a movie together. At times you may not feel loved but *know*

---

1 Warren W. Wiersbe, *Be Rich: Gaining the Things That Money Can't Buy* (Colorado Springs, CO: David C. Cook, 2009), 128.

*you are*. Every kind act, every glance, every embrace, every kiss, every word of encouragement can say I love you if you listen for it. If he comes home—he loves you. If she laid her head on a pillow next to yours—she loves you.

There is a time to talk through disappointments and struggles. This is called being vulnerable. Talking about feelings with an end goal of a stronger union and deeper understanding, cementing trust, will boost your marriage. This doesn't mean you talk about every little thing! And the men say, *Amen!* First, get your feelings under wraps and choose only the challenges you feel are threatening your marriage.

Intentionally and aggressively work on not allowing discussions to escalate. An escalating argument can be dangerous territory. Once nasty words are released from your mouth, you can never put them back. You can apologize, as you most certainly need to, but you can never erase damaging words. Even in a boxing match after three minutes the contenders go to their perspective corners to regroup and replenish. If things are getting overheated, ring the bell, and retreat to your corners *to pray*. God will refill, refocus, and replenish you. Then when you return to resolve your "match," you more than likely will be able to do so quickly, and with ease.

I've heard of couples staying up all night arguing, using "Be angry, and yet do not sin; do not let the sun go down on your anger, and do not give the devil an opportunity" (Ephesians 4:26–27). They take this passage to mean you've got to solve every conflict before going to bed. While, yes, this would be the best option—going to bed completely free of angst and turmoil—but a destructive choice if it means fighting all night.

You tell me, where's the fruit or benefit in this? Arguing all night? How can this help your relationship? Working through conflicts and getting to the other side *will* strengthen your marriage. It does not need to be all-out war.

So, what do you do?

You recognize you are not getting anywhere, acknowledge you are tired—*STOP*—and pick it up *later*, at a more agreeable time. This does not mean you are going to ignore working toward resolution. You set a time to resume your "discussion."Then you go to bed happy. You put your feelings on a shelf and focus on loving your spouse, trusting all will be resolved at your agreed-upon time. You can do this because you know he/she loves you and wants what's best for you. Acknowledge that fact, and go to sleep.

There are times when my husband and I are in a heated dispute and he says, "It's late, we're tired, let's pick this up tomorrow." In the morning we're laughing at how silly we had been the night before, and our "fight" is resolved in a matter of minutes. Moreover, Mike enacted a rule that we are not allowed to discuss charged issues after nine o'clock in the evening. If I inadvertently break the time rule and bring up a sensitive subject, he will look at his watch and say, "It's after nine." He loves this rule. I, on the other hand, am not as in love with it, but I know—without a doubt—it's best for our marriage. So, I grudgingly—*I mean, happily*—comply.

## Choose Love and Respect

Our feelings can be very deceptive. When we've been hurt or misunderstood, we are particularly vulnerable to our emotions taking over. If we act on a lie, which our feelings can tell us, such as, *He doesn't love me*, or *She doesn't really care about me*, or allow such thoughts to fester, we're treading in dangerous territory. It can cause all kinds of damage and turmoil in life. We *must* master our actions.

Elisabeth Elliot explains that our Creator has bestowed on us the capability to choose our actions; in scripture the heart *is* our free will. It's difficult to rein in our emotions, but we must not allow them to rule us. Never give your emotions authority over your life, especially in the area of romantic love. If we are to truly honor God, we must not allow our feelings to lead us.[2]

Scripture warns, "Above all else, guard your heart, for everything you do flows from it" (Proverbs 4:23 NIV).

Don't allow feelings to rule any day. We can choose to act in accordance with love and respect. Feed your brain with the truth of God's Word. We can choose what we allow our minds to think on.

On any given day you can select a verse from the Bible and say it over and over in your mind. Memorize verses to repeat to yourself when things begin to get heated, or even when life is *not* "heated" but wonderful. Choose from the list below or find some of your own.

Verses to meditate on:

---

2 Elisabeth Elliot, *Quest for Love* (Ada, MI: Revell Publishing, 2002), 35.

- "Set a guard, O LORD, over my mouth; keep watch over the door of my lips" (Psalm 141:3).
- "And the peace of God, which surpasses all comprehension, will guard your hearts and your minds in Christ Jesus" (Philippians 4:7).
- "An excellent wife, who can find? For her worth is far above jewels" (Proverbs 31:10).
- "She does him [her husband] good and not evil all the days of her life" (Proverbs 31:12).
- "My help comes from the LORD, who made heaven and earth. He will not allow your foot to slip; He who keeps you will not slumber" (Psalm 121:2–3).
- "'He who has found his life will lose it, and he who has lost his life for My sake will find it'" (Matthew 10:39).
- "A gentle answer turns away wrath, but a harsh word stirs up anger" (Proverbs 15:1).
- "Teach me to do Your will, for You are my God; let Your good Spirit lead me on level ground" (Psalm 143:10).
- "For the LORD God is a sun and shield; the LORD gives grace and glory; no good thing does He withhold from those who walk uprightly" (Psalm 84:11).
- "God is our refuge and strength, a very present help in trouble" (Psalm 46:1).
- "He gives strength to the weary, and to him who lacks might He increases power" (Isaiah 40:29).
- "Trust in the LORD with all your heart and do not lean on your own understanding. In all your ways

acknowledge Him, and He will make your paths
straight" (Proverbs 3:5–6).
- "'And you shall love the Lord your God with all your
heart, and with all your soul, and with all your mind,
and with all your strength'" (Mark 12:30).

# Discussion Questions

- Do you agree with the statement "We find what we look for"? Why or why not?

- Has there ever been a time when your feelings lied to you?

- Talk about a time when you were able to take control of negative emotions. How did you do this?

- Talk about a time when negative emotions took control of you.

- What do you think about the couple written about by Warren Wiersbe who got divorced and then re-married? What causes these types of actions?

- Discuss the idea of taking time-outs to pray when a discussion seems to be escalating. Do you think you can agree to follow this example?

- What do you think about the suggestion to memorize scripture in order to focus on God, and seeking His will? Is this something you think you would do?

# Chapter Seven
## Ladies, Don't Be His Mother; and Men, Learn to Stand Up to Yours

You're both in the car and he's driving. You pull into a parking lot. Simply pulling into a parking lot can turn into a stress-provoking affair. It's a catalyst for a potential fight. Why? You men probably already know. She's telling you where to park! You want to park where you want to. You want to hunt that spot down and conquer it! Raising your sword, you pull into the parking lot. Then the *love-of-your-life* aggressively points and navigates you through the lot while *criticizing* your parking skills. Deflated, you lower your sword.

Ladies, I get this! I understand the desire to help, because I happen to be married to *the worst parker in the world*! Searching for the perfect spot, he will often drive right past a car pulling out, forfeiting the spot to the car behind us. Sometimes I want to scream, "JUST PARK ALREADY!" But guess what? We've never gotten stuck in a parking lot. Ever. He always finds a spot, and he's never made us late because of his deficient parking talent. Interesting, isn't it?

Ladies, if he wants your assistance, he will ask for it. If he doesn't, be quiet. When he finally parks say, "Great spot." Repeat after me, "Great spot." Even if he passed a trillion other great spots. Even if he drove around for what seemed like an hour "hunting," or backed up multiple times because he wanted to park exactly between the lines. Even if you have a half-mile walk ahead of you to get to your destination. "Great spot." Since I'm married to the worst parker in the world and I can say it, you can, too.

He was parking way before he met you, and I'm sure he parks perfectly fine when you're not with him. I think he can handle parking the car without your assistance. Don't you?

Why is this so hard for us women? Why do we always want to assist and offer guidance? Because we are nurturers by nature. It's how God wired us. We are natural caregivers. We love, we protect, we support, we cherish, we *mother*. These are all noble and wonderful qualities. However, with your man, don't fall into the role of mothering him. It will be detrimental to the health of your marriage. Mother your children and your pets, but love and respect your husband.

Ladies, I am going to make this really clear for you. *No man wants to go to bed with his mother!* If you want to keep your marriage electric—*and hot and spicy*—don't try to be his mother. Chances are when he became a man he already knew how to put his big-boy pants on. He could have remained single, joined a monastery, or moved next door to Mommy. But he didn't. He chose you, because he wanted a wife. Be his wife!

How do you know if you're falling into mothering him? Any time you criticize him *like he's a child*. Or tell him what to do *like he's a child*. Or lecture him *like he's a child*. Or treat him *like he's a child.* Or belittle him *like he's a child.* You are acting like his mother. Don't. Do. It.

Moreover, never mock him in the bedroom or mock him about his bedroom abilities.

Dr. Kevin Leman states that men who are sexually fulfilled feel good about themselves and that a tremendous segment of a man's overall makeup is tied to how his wife responds to him sexually. Men want to be their wives' "hero" and lead her to "ecstasy." Conversely, the best way to emasculate a man is to ridicule him with regard to his *bedroom endeavors*. Act like he doesn't do anything for you sexually, and he *will* find a way to strike back at you.[1]

## Remember, You Are His Wife

Let me give you some examples:

He comes home after work, and you realize he forgot to pick up the molasses you needed for your special recipe.

Hands on hips. "Where's the molasses I asked you to get me?" you inquire.

"Oh, sweetheart, I totally forgot. I'm sorry."

"Well, I hope you like dry bread because I needed that molasses. How could you forget? This is the third time this week!"

Noooooo! Wrong. You're being his mother.

Instead:

"Okay, no problem. You can get it tomorrow."

1 Dr. Kevin Leman, *Sheet Music* (Carol Stream, IL: Tyndale House Publishers, 2003), 52.

Or better yet, if he keeps forgetting, maybe next time *get it yourself.*

Here's another example:

You ask him how his day was. He says he had to make some serious decisions about the future of the company he works for and who would be terminated. You ask for more information. After he tells you, you begin shooting off rapid-fire questions.

"Why did you say that?"

"Why did you let that person go and not the one who annoys you?"

"Why didn't you tell your boss to wait until after the holiday season?"

"Why. . .why. . .why. . . ?"

Noooooo! Stop it! Asking him why is like saying he did it wrong.

Instead:

"Your company is so fortunate to have you. I would have had a difficult time navigating all you did today. I'm so proud of you and the way you considered all aspects of the situation. Would you mind explaining a little bit more about your process in making such tough decisions?"

Here's another example:

He's been working a lot of overtime and you miss him.

When he gets home, you say with a scowl, "This is the third time this week you got home late. Is work really that important that you can't even call your wife? Why do you have to work so much overtime? I've hardly seen you all week!"

Nooooo! Would that motivate you to come home sooner? Would he want to come home to a wife who's on him like an angry gorilla? I think not!

Instead:

"I'm so glad you're home! I miss you. Is there any way we can spend more time together next week? You've been working so hard, and I appreciate all you do for us. Is there anything I can do to help you?"


Here's another example:

You're at a social gathering with friends or family. He's telling a story, but he's not telling it quite the way *you* remember it, and he's leaving out too many critical details. So you need to jump in. You say, "Well, that's not exactly how it happened. What happened was. . ."

Or he's speaking and you know the dryer stopped working on Tuesday and NOT Wednesday, so you have to correct his misinformation.

You say, "Wait, it wasn't Wednesday; I know it was Tuesday because that's the day we had chicken marsala for dinner."

Or he's telling the story *again* about how he got the best deal on his new car.

You say, "He's told that story so many times. I think the salespeople just wanted to turn over last year's inventory."

Or someone asks him a question, but you know the answer and can answer better than he can.

As he takes a breath you say, "Oh, I can answer that. . . ."

Noooooo! Really? Let the man speak for himself. What are you, his mother?

Don't be his mother. Be *the wife* who adores, cheers for, and builds up her man. Encourage him to raise his sword, and cheer as he defeats all the dragons.

A note to the men: Men, how do you address your lady if she's acting in a way that causes you to feel like you're being mothered or dishonored?

When you're alone, say something like this:

"Honey, please don't speak for me; it feels degrading. Or I feel belittled, put down, demeaned, when you speak to me like that. I love you, and I know you didn't mean to. But please stop. I don't like it."

If she accidentally does it again, you have another conversation. Calmly. Lovingly. It is critical that you have these conversations. Failure to lovingly communicate with your wife and instead choosing to withdraw will be detrimental to the overall health of your marriage. A woman will respect a man who will stand up for what he believes is right, even if this means you don't agree with her or are addressing her unwanted behavior.

## Criticizing Cuts

Ladies, when you criticize your man, what he hears is *"I don't trust you. I don't respect you. I don't think you're doing it right."* Always treat him like he's the smartest, most capable man in the world.

Much of what we've been talking about can fall under the category of nagging. No man likes to be nagged. How do you define *nagging*? Nagging can be defined as whatever he considers nagging. If he feels as though he's being nagged—then he's being nagged.

The Bible describes this as a contentious woman: "It is better to live in a corner of the roof than in a house shared with a contentious woman" (Proverbs 25:24). Let me further define *contentious* for you: Argumentative, combative, quarrelsome, naysaying, belligerent—nagging. Any time you tumble into such behavior you dishonor God, and you dishonor your marital vows. This is one of Satan's traps for women, and I've been prey to it myself. What's a girl to do if this happens? Apologize and start over.

He *needs* your respect. God commands, ". . .and the wife must see to it that she respects her husband" (Ephesians 5:33). When God commands something, He means business, and we need to follow what He says if we want to have a flourishing, God-honoring marriage. And this command stands even when your man may be wandering from God's best: "In the same way, you wives, be submissive to your own husbands so that even if any of them are disobedient to the word, they may be won without a word by the behavior of their wives, as they observe your chaste and respectful behavior" (1 Peter 3:1–2).

As soon as you take on the role of critic, your marriage will be on shaky ground. God has wired a man in such a way that he—*seeks, needs, longs for*—the approval of his wife. When your respect for him wanes, it cuts him to the core.

(Men, can I get anyone to second this? Agree or disagree, express how you feel on this one, men.)

When a wife loses respect for her husband, the marriage is in grave danger.


## Saying No

Another way a woman takes on a mommy role is by "punishing" him when he says no to a request.

As in, "Can you pick up squash on your way home?"

Or, "Can we go shopping tonight for my mom's birthday gift?"

Or, "Would you help me decorate these cookies for my luncheon?"

Or, "Would you come with me while I try on thirty pairs of shoes but don't buy any?"

"I'm so tired. I'd rather not."

"Fine!" And then he gets the cold shoulder all night.

Grown men need to be able to say no in a relationship. In fact, saying no flows back and forth in a healthy marriage. If we can't say no, then our yes doesn't mean a whole lot. How can we really say yes if no is not an option without repercussion? Stop and think about this. If you get mad at him for saying no, guess what? *Mommy, again.*

Let him have the power to say no. Women need this same freedom as well. Ladies, having said this, I also want to caution you greatly against saying no to a request for sex. Suggested alternate answers are *Can it be quick? Later today? Tomorrow?* But a flat-out no is ill-advised. We will talk more about this in chapter ten. Stay tuned! We're going to have some fun! Men, don't flip to chapter ten now. Stay with me; what we are about to discuss is important if you want to "have fun" on a regular basis. But before we move on, ladies, listen from a man's perspective: Dr. Kevin Leman equates a man needing sexual release to getting kicked *there*, stating that it really can be painful.[2]

Enough said on this for now.

## Love Her

Shall we switch to the men now? And you ladies say, *Finally!*

Men, another time the marriage is in grave danger is when she feels unloved. A married woman who is unloved is a very vulnerable woman. Feeling unloved leaves any woman with empty desires and voracious longing. Reassure her of your love daily with "I love you" and acts of adoration. Cherish. Her. Always.

Consider how strongly the Bible addresses an unloved married woman: "Under three things the earth quakes, and under four, it cannot bear up: Under a slave when he becomes king, and a fool when he is satisfied with food, *under an unloved woman when she gets a husband*, and a maidservant when she supplants her mistress" (Proverbs 30:21–23, emphasis added).

LOVING your wife is putting her above all others *including your mother*. Earlier I quoted Ephesians 5:33 about wives respecting their husbands; the beginning of this

---

2 Ibid., 147.

verse starts with, "Nevertheless, each individual among you also is to love his own wife even as himself" (Ephesians 5:33).

Love your wife. Do everything in your power so she never questions your love for her. If Mom gives you a plaque reading HOME IS WHERE YOUR MOM IS, kindly *give it back.* When a wife feels second to "Mommy," she can feel unloved. Never give her reason for this.

*Of course my wife comes before my mother,* I can hear you men scoffing, *you don't have to tell me this!*

Let me ask you: Can you say no to your mother?

For example:

You're out to dinner with your wife, and your mom calls. Naturally, you answer the phone, right?

No! This is one surefire way to give her reason to feel second to Mom. If you're with your wife, *you are with your wife.* If you feel you must respond to your mom, let your wife know you're telling Mom you will call her tomorrow or later. You can do this with a text message. Or even better, don't bring your phone to dinner with you, and instead focus completely on your wife.

You have a date night planned with your wife and your mom wants to come along. I mean, Mom is lonely; let her come along, right?

What? No! Are you kidding me? What does this communicate to your wife? She will probably tell you, "Oh, it's okay if your mom joins us," because she loves you and wants to please you *and* your mom. But DON'T DO IT! Date nights are for you and your wife. You tell Mom *no,* and don't even ask your wife. You can make plans with Mom for another time.

Your mom invites you and your wife to Sunday brunch. You accept the invitation immediately upon her sweet request.

No matter how sweetly your mom asks you, you don't agree to an invitation *for your wife* without asking your wife first.

Mom needs you to watch her cocker spaniel while she goes on vacation. You bring Frederico home even though your wife is allergic to dogs. She can take allergy medicine, right?

Wrong! Does this really need an explanation?

You're on your way home from work. This can be a perfect time to call Mom to catch up. When you arrive home, you continue the conversation in the house even though your wife is home.

I don't think so. Get off the phone before you go inside! Don't be on the phone with your mother, or anyone for that matter, when you greet your loving wife. My married son will often call me on his drive home from work. As he pulls into his garage, he says, "Okay, well, I'm home now." I know this means he is hanging up, and rightly so!

Your mom has a habit of calling early in the morning and waking you both up. It's your mom, so you just put up with it.

Na-na-na-na-no! Have a discussion with Mom and let her know what time is acceptable. (This would apply for any friend or family member, too, by the way.)

Mom lives in another state and wants to come for a visit.

She informs you of her travel arrangements. You give your wife the dates so she can mark the calendar and have your home ready.

Are you serious? Mom (or any family member) needs to check with you, *and your wife*, before arriving for a visit. Any time I visit my adult children, I ask for permission; barging in would violate their home. Let Mom know she needs to ask first. And always check with your wife.

Your mom accidentally criticizes your wife. She doesn't mean to, but it seems to happen every time you get together. Just ignore it. Why would you want to start pandemonium? Right? Plus, if you said anything, it may cause Mom to cry. You wouldn't want to do that.

Gentlemen, come on! No! Really? You can't just ignore your mother's critiques of your wife. Address her. Say something like this: "Mom, I know you don't mean to, however, I've heard you criticizing my wife, and I need you to stop."

## Honor Your Parents

*Doesn't the Bible teach us to honor our parents?* Yes, absolutely! However, you can honor your parents *and* still put your spouse first. For example, when my son was dating his wife, he was in the car with her and her parents while they were on their way to dinner. I called, and he didn't answer his phone. They were a bit surprised he didn't answer when *Mom* called.

This sent a message to his future wife: she would not be pushed aside every time Mom "rang." I was proud of him and expected nothing less. He called me back *the next day*.

If it had been a serious issue, I would have left a message or texted him. If it were an emergency, I would have dialed 911 and *not* my son.

Honoring your parents does not mean you're *always* available for them when *they* want you to be available. I have a close relationship with all of my adult children, and I completely understand they are not going to be available every time I want them to be available.

To further illustrate the balance between honoring your parents while putting your spouse first, consider the following story.

Doug and Sue were newly married when Doug's mom passed away. Before she died, Doug promised her he'd take care of his dad, Charlie, adding, "He'll be no big problem for me." His mom warned, "I wish for your sake it was going to be me left, because he's not easy!" Doug thought it was funny and a bit absurd. In spite of his mom's seemingly silly warning—*honoring his dad*—Doug moved Charlie into their home.

It didn't take long before he fully realized why his mom would give him such forewarning. Charlie didn't follow "house rules." He allowed his dogs to roam and didn't clean up their "messes," and he also left his own "messes." Doug calmly talked with him about each infraction, but Charlie wouldn't budge. The worst part was when Charlie disrespected Sue by calling her obscenities. Doug would say to his dad, "You can't call my wife that." But again, Charlie wouldn't change. "I had to move him out," Doug told me. Respecting his wife and honoring his dad at the same time,

Doug rented a room nearby for Charlie.

Years later when Charlie was dying, and they got the call that he wouldn't make it another day, Doug couldn't bear to watch his father pass. Sue was the one to spend Charlie's last day with him, staying with Charlie from 8:00 a.m. until he passed away at 7:00 p.m. As Sue reflected back on the experience: "There were things I did wrong, too. I provoked Charlie in many ways. It wasn't easy being there at the end, but I knew I needed to. Doug just couldn't."

Doug honored his dad *and* his wife, and at the end of Charlie's life, Sue extended double honor to Doug's dad. She stepped up with love and compassion and did what was unbearable for Doug.


## Breaking It Down

Be cautious about your approach when you decide to talk with your mom about various occurrences. You never want your mom to think your wife petitioned you to talk with her. You want your mom and your wife to have a vibrant relationship, true? It's always better to have a talk with Mom *before* your wife says anything to you. Step up and take action before it becomes an issue between you and your wife. Then, if and when your wife asks you about said incident, you can say, "I already talked with my mom about this, and I trust she will do better in the future. I'm sorry 'such and such' happened."

You want her to respect you as a man—so be proactive. Establishing healthy communication with your mom will give your beloved wife reason to praise you. Do you remember my story with my son in chapter two just before he got married and I had visualized an *alone* day together? Do you recall his words? "Mom, suck it up! She is going to be my wife. She's coming with us." He never told her about our "talk," and I'm happy to say I've never given him reason to say those words to me again. However, when I decided to write about it, I told my daughter-in-law about said incident. She told me she thought Tim could have been a lot nicer with his approach, adding, "Suck it up" was a bit harsh. Personally, I thought it was perfect because it caused me to check myself and make a U-turn. Men, sometimes you need to teach your mom how to be a good mother-in-law.

And now, we are on to examples of when you most likely need to have a talk with Mom. Ready? One, two, three. . .jump!

You bring your fiancée to your mother's home and Mom has pictures displayed of you and an old girlfriend or ex-wife. Oh my! Take Mom aside as soon as possible and ask her to remove the pictures. If she refuses, inform her you will not be coming for visits until she does.

Mom likes to regularly impart her wisdom on your wife, giving her unsolicited advice on how to be a wife and, after children arrive, how to parent. Along with said advice, words are spoken that hurt your wife's feelings. Gulp! If Mom carelessly or unintentionally insults your wife, you need to address it.

If your mom regularly excludes your wife, you need to have a talk with Mom about how hurtful it is to be left out. (She probably didn't even realize she was doing so. If, by chance, she was ignoring and/or dismissing your wife on purpose, you've got a more serious problem to address. But here's a hint: put your wife first.)

On the opposite spectrum, if your mom is showing up unannounced to your residence, this needs to be addressed—by YOU! Let your mom know she needs to ASK for permission to visit. And Mom needs to be gracious if your wife, or you, tells her no. It's not okay for her to pop in. Protect your wife.

When there are family events, your mom needs to ask if you and your wife would like to attend. Any time Mom commands or dictates "rules," whether spoken or unspoken, you need to have a talk with her. For instance, let's say there's an upcoming family wedding in another state and your mom *expects* you both to be there. You and your wife need to decide what events you attend; Mom can ask but never manipulate or demand you attend. If you decide to pass on this wedding and your mom gives your wife grief over it, *you need to address her*. Any time your mom tries to dictate your schedule, it's time for you to have a talk with her. Your wife needs to be sheltered from this sort of manipulation—addressing Mom is *your* job.

If your mom is ever rude or unkind to your wife, don't ignore rudeness. Gently let her know it will not be tolerated. Be kind but firm.

Keep in mind that the goal is to have healthy extended family relationships where family can love and support one another.

Although the above examples are for a son with his mom,

they can be applied to all extended relationships. Look out for your spouse and put him/her first. Before, you only had to look out for you, but after you commit to marriage you need to think about *WE*.

## Be Kind

I wish writing this next section wasn't necessary. But I've heard horrible stories about wives being disrespectful and unkind to their husband's mom. Ladies, please always be kind and courteous. Perhaps these women felt "second to Mommy" and inadvertently lashed out. Even if this was true, it's never acceptable to be unkind to your spouse's extended family. When you love someone, you love whom he or she loves—or at the very least are kind and considerate.

Men, if your wife is ever mean or disrespectful to your mom, I would hope you'd gently talk with her. Ask why. My guess would be it's because she may be feeling uncertain of your love for her or insecure about your relationship with your mom. Never shy away from addressing discourteous behavior. Any godly woman will receive such loving correction, and in turn, her admiration for you will increase.

Ladies, on the same note, never accept negative words or actions toward or about your husband from your mom or extended family members. Let your mom know you will not listen to complaints about your husband. Ever. In turn, refrain from negative, critical talk about the "new family" you married into. This can be very hurtful and damaging to your family and overall interpersonal health. Again, the love and support of family can be one of the greatest blessings to your life together. We were not designed to do "family" alone, which is why it is critical to establish healthy communication and interaction. Parents, siblings, grandparents, aunts, uncles. . .can greatly enrich your life and the prosperity and happiness of your marriage.

Switching from *ME* to *WE* introduces new family dynamics; and establishing nurturing interaction with each other and extended family will set you up for a thriving, loving, flourishing marriage. (We will discuss more on this subject in the next chapter.)

# Discussion Questions

- Men, what would be your definition of *nagging*? Ladies, how do you feel about his definition?

- What does it feel like for you when he/she criticizes you?

- How would you define *respect*? What does respecting each other look like to you?

- Consider this quote from the chapter: "If we can't say no, then our yes doesn't mean a whole lot." Do you agree or disagree? Why?

- How do you feel about using the word *no*? How difficult is it for you to say no to your mom or your dad? How difficult is it for you to say no to each other?

- How difficult is it for you to hear the word *no*?

# Chapter Eight
## Expectations and Establishing Your Family

I was born into a big Italian family. So much of the way my family operated centered on, and around, food. Gathering for "feasts" was love in action. Choosing not to participate was ancestral homicide. After my husband and I got married, it was expected that he would accompany me to my parents' house *every* Sunday, for Sunday night dinner. And that's what we did.

This family institution had been handed down through the generations. It's what you did if you were in my family. No questions. No aforethought. No complaints. No qualms. You didn't have to add it to your calendar events—it was already there—with invisible marker etched in your schedule.

Through the years, even after our kids were born, guess where we were on Sunday evenings? You got it! My parents' house, stuffing our faces with mostaccioli, ricotta cheese, bread sticks, meatballs, and cannoli. Sounds delicious, right? And it was, but here's the problem: I never asked Mike if going to my parents' house *every* Sunday was something *he* wanted to do. I never asked my husband if it was a tradition he wanted to continue with *our family*. We never talked about it. Ever. We just went. Why didn't Mike ever question this expectation? Simply put, he grew up in a home where you didn't question what was expected of you. Opposing the rules was unheard of. He took what he knew, I took what I knew, and we *just did* without questioning what *we* wanted for *our family*. (More on this ancestral saga later.)

This is what we do; we go into marriage with unspoken expectations and rules. We enter with unspoken needs and desires. We enter with our own set of "rules" for our new family, which we learned from our family of origin.

It's time to pause and reflect. What were your family traditions? Which did you like? Which did you dislike? How many of those do you want to continue? What was your own parents' marriage like? Are you expecting your marriage to be as theirs was? Do you want it to be?

In this chapter we're going to question what many of you, while growing up, were not allowed to question. We're going to question the way your family operated and if it's the way you want to function as you establish your new family. The moment you say "I do," your new family is birthed; and with it, you get to birth the way your family will function. There may be many practices, beliefs, and procedures your parents did that you'll want to repeat. But there may be many family patterns you want to break. And this is okay. This is *your* family and you get to make the rules now. Going from *ME* to *WE* means disconnecting from your extended family and designing your new family. Your extended family can still be a huge part of your life, to whatever degree you choose, but your primary concern and priority needs to be your new life together.

## Game-of-Life Violations

Just like in a basketball game when the referee calls a foul, you need to call a foul when your parents *demand* anything from you. You are an adult—with your own family—and adults *ask*; they don't *tell* each other what to do. Parents need to request what they desire of you.

I'll give you an example from my life:

After my daughter got married, I told my son-in-law to mark his calendar for Christmas Eve brunch at his new in-laws' house. I thought I was including him and being kind. On Christmas Eve he and my daughter did arrive as instructed, but they were an hour late and arrived looking like they were on their way to the gym—*not* a holiday celebration. The tension toward me was clear. If I'm going to be honest, I felt hurt. I felt hurt they were late. I felt hurt they didn't seem to want to be with us. I felt hurt they put a blemish on my Christmas Eve tradition. Did you catch that? *My* tradition. Later, when I asked my daughter about what had happened, she said, "Mom, you never asked us if we wanted to join you." She was 100 percent right! And it was her way of letting me know *You're not allowed to boss me around anymore!* The next year I *asked* if they wanted to join us. They both said they would love to, and we had a completely different experience. I was totally wrong and had to apologize and do an about-face.

New families are a learning curve for everyone. This can be an instance where the roles are reversed with you teaching your parents how to be good in-laws.

My husband and I have a good relationship with our three adult children and their families. They welcome our involvement in their lives because we follow their rules and terms. They made the rules for their new family. *You* make the rules for *your* new family.

## Your Family Ship

Think of it like a ship in the middle of a bay. You control your own ship—your new family. You decide when you leave the ship, where you go, whom you interact with, who boards your ship, when someone boards your ship and how long they stay, and what objects are allowed on your ship. Your new family—*your ship*—is surrounded by a body of water protecting you from outsiders. If anyone wants to visit, they need permission to board. Just like in Acts 27:18—"they began to jettison the cargo," as in, throw overboard—you may need to jettison excess "baggage" in order to keep your ship healthy and floating.

Men, you are the captain of your ship; don't give up your God-given position to *anyone*. Not your mother-in-law, not your mom, dad, father-in-law, friends. . .no one. Ponder this: "But I want you to understand that Christ is the head of every man, and the man is the head of a woman, and God is the head of Christ" (1 Corinthians 11:3).

I heard of a situation with a newly married couple named

John and Sandy. They had a friend, Tyler, who would visit on a regular basis. Tyler traveled for work as a salesperson and would visit John and Sandy every time he was in their town. The couple wanted to be gracious hosts and accommodated him. The problem was, Tyler never asked to visit but instead informed them when he'd be making an appearance *at their home*. After he arrived, Tyler would dictate much of the schedule. And not only this, he would also make dinner requests of Sandy and would complain when he didn't like meals or anything else he found displeasing. I mean, doesn't the Bible say to be hospitable? "Be hospitable to one another without complaint" (1 Peter 4:9). John and Sandy were being as gracious as possible.

Yes, we are to be hospitable to one another, *but* we decide when we allow someone on our ship, and when he or she leaves. Finally, John got tired of the way Tyler was showing up with expectations, dictating, and not honoring their home. John nicely put Tyler "in a lifeboat and gave it a push." Basically, limits were set with Tyler regarding when he was *invited* to visit and how long his stay lasted; he wasn't allowed to barge in anymore.

Extended family and friends need permission to board your family ship.

My husband and I adhere to our adult children's "ship" rules, and they adhere to ours as well. My kids know if they are on the phone with me when their dad gets home, I will be hanging up. My kids know I will put their dad's needs before theirs. My kids know they need to knock on our door if they come over. (Yes, marriage can stay spicy even after thirty or

131

forty years!) If they want to visit and stay overnight, they ask—just like we ask them. We *all* ask for what we desire from one another, and we *all* have the freedom to say no when we feel it's necessary. This is how we respect one another as adults. As a universal rule, we extend the same courtesy we want ourselves.

Please understand I am not at all suggesting you create an island around you, keeping yourselves isolated. On the contrary, connecting with family and friends is an important part of emotional health. Let others in on a regular basis, and deepen your lives with loved ones who are in your corner. Especially when children are born—grandparents and aunts and uncles can play a critical part in overall contentment and both spiritual and emotional growth. There is a huge difference between letting others be a part of your lives, which I highly recommend, and allowing others to have control over your lives.

## Gifts

Another way I've seen captains lose control of their family ship is when in-laws give "gifts" with perceived expectations. In other words, *"We bought this for you, and in return we expect such and such from you."* The new car comes with limits and instructions on who gets to drive it. The vacation comes with the expectation you will be at every family gathering. The help with the down payment for your house comes with expectations the extended family can stay anytime they choose to. The list goes on and on until the gift givers are in control of your family ship.

Only allow gifts on your ship that have no demands attached and are truly gifts. A true gift is freely given—you can do whatever you choose with the gift, and you don't have to do anything in return for the gift.

## Leading

Men, always be the point man for your home—your family, your wife, and your children. You are the guard and leader of your family: "For the husband is the head of the wife, as Christ also is the head of the church, He Himself being the Savior of the body" (Ephesians 5:23).

Author Elisabeth Elliot contrasts Jesus' leadership over the Church to a man's leadership in his family. For a man to reject this God-ordained leadership and authority is disobedience to the Father. Henceforth, when a wife is in opposition to her husband's leadership, she is in opposition to God. A man submits to Christ when he steps into his position of headship in his family. Christ displayed His willingness as head over the Church as He exemplified submission to the Father, which is our ultimate example.[1]

Who will lead? Men, are you going to abdicate your God-given role and become passive? Most women respect a strong man who leads well. She may seem to want to take the reins, but make no mistake about it, a woman will respect a man who will not allow her to push him around.

In the movie *Take the Lead*, released in 2006, Antonio Banderas plays the internationally known dancer Pierre

---

1 Elisabeth Elliot, *The Mark of a Man* (Ada, MI: Fleming H. Revell, 2007), 105.

Dulaine. Pierre teaches ballroom dance to New York City public-school teenagers, and there are two scenes from that movie I absolutely love.

Allow me to set the stage: A young man, Rock, and a young lady, LaRhette, who have been rivals, both find themselves in trouble and under Mr. Dulaine's instruction. As a form of "discipline," Mr. Dulaine instructs the students to dance together.

Mr. Dulaine: Please, take the dancing position.
Please...come on.
(They take their respective ballroom dance positions.)
Mr. Dulaine: Let's see this. We are just going to move, very simply. Let's just, uh, walk.
(LaRhette begins to push and shove Rock. Mr. Dulaine stops her.)
Mr. Dulaine: No no no. LaRhette, the man leads. It is the woman's job to follow.
LaRhette: Oh, so if he gets to lead, then he's gonna think he's boss?
Mr. Dulaine: No, but he's not. You see, the man proposes the step. It is the woman's choice to accept by following. Now, to follow takes as much strength as to lead. Good? All right. Let's do it again. Come on, come on! Now, Rock, just walk. Just forward, just walking. Yeah, forward. Just walking, like that. Here you go. Yeah, you know how to walk. Now walk back. There you go.
You're dancing, you're dancing. . . .

And then, in a later scene. . .

Mr. Dulaine: The Waltz. It cannot be done without trust between partners.
LaRhette: Well, then it's just not gonna happen.
Mr. Dulaine: But trust must be earned, LaRhette.
Rock: Good luck with that.
Mr. Dulaine: All right, I have something here that is gonna help.
(He takes off his tie and places it over her eyes.)
LaRhette: Don't put that thing on my eyes!
Mr. Dulaine: I'm asking you to do something very courageous.
LaRhette: Besides dance with him?
Mr. Dulaine: There. Come on. Now Rock, you have the. . .over here. You have the opportunity to use every bit of strength and skill you possess, not to dominate her, but to take her on a journey. It is a lot to ask. If and how you take the journey. . .that's entirely up to you.
(He leaves the room.)
LaRhette: (blindfolded) He's gone?
Rock: Yeah. You down?
LaRhette: I guess.
(Rock begins to move.)
LaRhette: Wrong way. You always start forward and I start back.
Rock: All right, yeah. I can figure it out.
LaRhette: I'm just trying to help.

Rock: I wish he'd tie that thing around your mouth.
You ready or what?
LaRhette: Okay.
Rock: Okay.
LaRhette: O-kay.
Rock: I saw that.
LaRhette: What?!
Rock: What are you smiling for?
LaRhette: Shut up, I'm not.
Rock: All right, you're not.

Ladies, are you willing to trust God by trusting your husband? To trust is to be courageous. I ask you, which is harder, to lead or to trust? In Proverbs 21:1 it says, "The king's heart is like channels of water in the hand of the LORD; He turns it wherever He wishes." Any time you are having trouble with trust, insert your husband's name for "king" and let that settle in for a while.

To trust does not mean you are void of an opinion, quite the contrary. When we, as women, withhold our knowledge and insight, we withhold who we are. It is a foolish man who ignores the wisdom of his wife. However, just as Rock said in the movie scene, "I wish he'd tie that thing around your mouth," oftentimes, the wisest action is silence. A man is not to dominate his wife, absolutely not! A godly man offers leadership through loving her, cherishing her, and looking out for her.

And yet, at the same time, we need to be mindful that even the best of men are still merely men. Never look to a man to fulfill only that which God can. When a woman chooses to place herself under her husband's leadership, she is not only trusting her husband; she is trusting God, and in doing so, yields out of respect and trust. Ladies, will you trust him?

## Holidays

As holidays roll in, the potential for conflict rolls in as well. Many newly married couples have some of their most poignant fights over where they will go for the various holidays. *We want to be fair*, a phrase I've heard often. Before you talk about what's *fair*, have a discussion about what you both *want*. Take turns expressing what each of you would like most, listening to the other without judgment or defensiveness. After both of you have had a chance to describe what the ideal scenario would be, then figure out how to mold both of your desires. It may be you both want the same thing.

There was one couple who vehemently argued over traveling for Christmas. Her family lived in another state, and she always traveled home for Christmas. Finally he asked, "Do you *want to* travel to Boston for Christmas?" She thought about it and then said, "No. I really don't want to." He said, "Then why are we arguing?" They both wanted the same thing but were arguing over what seemed "fair."

The first step is to figure out what you both want and see how many of those desires line up. Then, figure out how to be fair with each other. Some couples go to one family for Thanksgiving and the other for Christmas and then switch the following year. Many of you have parents who are divorced, and therefore have to navigate multiple requests. What some have done is inform their families they will be staying home, and then invite extended family and friends to their home. The important thing is to decide together and have a plan.

## Traditions

In the beginning of our marriage when holidays arrived, my husband and I did what was expected of us and didn't question "the system." It wasn't until many years and two kids later that we sat down with *our family* and decided together what our holidays and family traditions would be. For too many years, we floated around trying to please our extended family and never talked about establishing our own family traditions. We needed to have this conversation before we were married, and finally, when we did, we set out a plan that is still intact today.

One custom we started is what we fondly call Family Night. Every Friday night was dedicated to being together as a family. As our kids got older they were given the option to participate or not. When the teenage years approached, we fully expected they would choose to be with friends instead of with us during our Friday Family Night ritual. To our surprise, they enjoyed our Family Night just as much as we did, and not only joined us as teenagers but as adults as well.

When one of our sons was a teenager, there was a Friday afternoon when a group of his friends stopped by our house and invited him to play a game at a local park. He happily joined in. Just before dinner the group came back to our house. We heard his friends say good-bye to him. I asked him where they were going. He told me they were going to one of their friend's houses to get pizza and watch movies. Feeling bad my son wasn't included, I asked, "Why didn't you join them?" What he said shocked me. "Mom, it's Family Night."

At my daughter's eighteenth birthday party, one of her friends announced, "We all knew Monica wasn't available on Friday night because it was Family Night."

My other son, who lives in another state, has established Family Night with his own family.

When my husband and I started this family tradition, we had no idea how it would profoundly impact our family legacy. It all started with a talk and a plan and then a commitment to carry it through week after week. Without question, this ritual was one of the best decisions we made as a family.

## What about You?

Jen and Mark had saved for years for their dream vacation to Hawaii. As the trip approached, Jen dreamed of days on the beach soaking up the sun. Mark imagined fun adventures and seeing as much of beautiful Hawaii as he possibly could.

As Mark's Hawaii travel brochures began piling up and Jen noticed he'd written on each, mapping out his course, she realized they might not be envisioning the same magical escape. She wanted to keep her feet planted in the sand, while he wanted to be the ultimate incessantly roaming Hawaiian tourist. When more and more travel brochures kept flooding in, Jen knew she needed to talk with him about what they both desired for their vacation. After talking and agreeing to a plan, they decided to alternate days between sightseeing and relaxing on the beach. Having a plan saved their trip. This may have led to huge Hawaii fights, with the potential to ruin their dream vacation, if they hadn't talked and agreed to a plan.

Your marriage is way more important than a trip to Hawaii. Sharing your hopes and dreams with each other, as well as having a plan, will set you up for success. Now, think about your future as husband and wife. What are the traditions, rules, customs, and habits you want to establish? What are you envisioning with regard to married life?

You may be anticipating an endless sea of sexual bliss. Or imagining long talks every morning while watching the sun rise and drinking coffee together. You need to talk about your expectations and hopes.

You also need to talk about the day-to-day operation of your home. Discuss the bathrooms, which will need cleaning, the floors that will need scrubbing, the dirty clothes, dusty dressers, grimy windows, and soiled carpet. Don't forget the kitchen and the food cooking, prep, shopping, and cleanup.

How will you divide the space in your bedroom? One couple—after ten years of marriage—discovered during counseling that he started each day with angry feelings toward his wife. She had the majority of storage space in their bedroom, leaving him with only one drawer. He became increasingly bitter as he rummaged through his single drawer of clothes each morning. This went on for ten years! You need to talk about this stuff!

Are you messy? Think about who will be doing the clean-up and who needs to be more conscientious about leaving messes. Who will do the cooking? Who will take care of the maintenance on the cars?

For years my husband quietly endured dealing with our bedroom looking like a going-out-of-business-shoe-store-sale. I thought it was so sweet when I'd find my shoes organized and lined up in our closet. I'd thank him but then go right back to leaving my shoes haphazardly scattered throughout our bedroom.

One day he tripped on one of my shoes in our bedroom, launching him toward the headboard on our bed, leaving him with a sprained ankle. This motivated Mike to have a discussion with me about "the shoes." I seriously had no idea it bothered him. Feel free to shout, *"Clueless!"* After apologizing, I gave it my all to keep the shoes put away. After we talked about it, I changed. Today there are no shoes on the floor in our bedroom.

Keeping your home clean can become an issue if you don't set up guidelines. Jack grew up in a home where weekends were marked for family adventures and having fun. Carly's family would clean on the weekends. As the weekends approached, Jack expected to have fun, while Carly expected to clean their house. As you can imagine, this caused quite a bit of friction. Finally, they had a discussion and decided they would hire someone to clean their home, which would enable them to enjoy their weekends together.

If you both are planning to work, you need to distribute the family chores and responsibilities. Do you plan on having children? This is another discussion you need to have. Many families carry on as a two-income family after kids arrive, and others like one parent to be home. Have a plan in place as your family grows.

Mike and I both worked and saved as much as possible because we knew when children arrived, I would stay home. For us, it was the best family decision we ever made.

Talk about toothpaste, dishes, cooking, housework, drawer space, furniture, dirty clothes, electronics, and anything else you need to fit in your combined space. One couple I know has separate bathrooms. It works for them. You need to figure out what will work for you.

## Family Map

What do you want to establish for the way your family operates? What are your core values? What are the family rules? An excellent way to map this out would be to construct a Family Mission Statement. There will be many decisions and choices made over many years. When your priorities are clear, your direction will be easily decided. What do you value most?

A Family Mission Statement is a written statement proclaiming your core values as a family. The most well-known

Family Mission Statement is found in Joshua 24:15. "...but as for me and my house, we will serve the LORD."

As King David was dying he passed down what one could call a Family Mission Statement:

*As David's time to die drew near, he charged Solomon his son, saying, "I am going the way of all the earth. Be strong, therefore, and show yourself a man. Keep the charge of the LORD your God, to walk in His ways, to keep His statutes, His commandments, His ordinances, and His testimonies, according to what is written in the Law of Moses, that you may succeed in all that you do and wherever you turn, so that the LORD may carry out His promise which He spoke concerning me, saying, 'If your sons are careful of their way, to walk before Me in truth with all their heart and with all their soul, you shall not lack a man on the throne of Israel.'"*

—1 KINGS 2:1–4

Here's our Williams Family Mission Statement:

*The Williams Family puts God as top priority. We serve God and each other. We have unconditional love for all family members. We listen, forgive, help up, stand up, defend, and work as a team. Our home will be a place of refuge where we honor each other, laugh a lot, and don't take ourselves too seriously.*

Your Family Mission Statement is entirely up to you. You can start with one and change it as your family grows. Make it personal to your family. I highly recommend writing one together and placing it in a strategic place in your home.

# Discussion Questions

- How do you feel about what the author said about men being the captain of the family ship? Do you agree or disagree?

- What does it mean to be the captain of your ship?

- What makes you feel loved?

- Discuss how you will divide the household chores.

- What are your thoughts about submission?

- What's the difference between letting others in your life versus letting others have control in your life?

- Schedule a time to sit down together and write your own Family Mission Statement.

# Chapter Nine
## You Can Have Sex Now

One young lady who had never been with a man once told me, "Penises scare me."

Rightly so! If you've never seen one or touched one, it's an entirely natural response.

Where can engaged couples go for straight talk about what to expect on their wedding night? Come on, we know it's what you think about more often than you'd like to admit to your mother. Let's get it all out there! I think we need to talk about this, don't you?

You are about to venture into the unfamiliar world of marriage where everything feels exhilarating. Except maybe going over your guest list again.

This chapter will be straight talk from a "mom." Everything here is what I told my own kids, so it's right from the heart.

Since I know you're thinking about this, we are jumping right in. Let's talk about when sex goes from no to GO!

### The Wedding Night
You've got the scene all mapped out. You both barely make it into your room, kissing all the way there. The passion roars

as you devour each other with unyielding thirst. Once in the room, half of your clothes are already off as the sexual electricity builds, and when you finally make it to the bed you feel magic. Mystical. Ecstasy.

Fantasy.

Please. Stop watching all of those movies! If you want magic and mystical, take a trip to Disneyland and eat ice cream together as you stare at the castle and all the pretty lights.

Most engaged couples have high expectations for their wedding night, but the truth of the matter is many have been terribly disappointed, left with a mediocre or bad memory. For some, it's a memory they wish they could erase. However, it does not have to be that way for you! I want it to be an amazing experience—no, *beyond amazing*—for you, one you will replay in your mind with excitement for many years to come.

But first let me share some stories with you so you don't think I'm making this stuff up!


## Comin' Up Short

While at a gathering of pastors' wives, Tracy—young, new to the group, and recently married to a pastor—blurted out to all of us, "That's it?! That's what I've been waiting for?" Of course, she was referring to her much-awaited physical relationship with her husband. Tracy went on to say she was trying to be a good wife by not turning him down sexually. She was responding to his advances with, "Again?

Okay, come on...(sigh)...let's go." For her, it was just going through the motions. Not really getting much out of it. She talked about it like one would talk about doing the dishes or cleaning the bathroom.

Men, I know that's not at all what you want from your bride.

Dr. Kevin Leman tells a story from the husband's perspective about a newly married couple—both virgins—on their wedding night. This new groom wanted everything to be perfect and beautiful. He thought he was being careful and gentle—and moving along slowly. But she started crying. Being considerate, he stopped. Then he ran a bath for her, hoping it would relax her. He even knew what her favorite scent was and ran out and bought it for her. Even the lavender scent didn't help! In exchange for the magical night he had envisioned, he got to listen to his bride sobbing in the bathroom tub. And if that weren't enough, with the aroma of lavender escaping from the bathroom, he heard her call her mom. She talked with her mom for two hours.[1]

Ladies, please don't call your mom on your wedding night. Please!

Author Marla Taviano details a friend's nightmare of a wedding night. Upon leaving their reception, as they arrived at their hotel, Amanda was consumed with amorous passion. She had left her wedding dress on, along with her tiara and high-heel shoes, as part of her *sensual strategy* for their first *romantic* night together. Amanda had envisioned Nathan taking her out of her wedding attire as part of her plan of a

---

1 Dr. Kevin Leman, *Under the Sheets* (Ada, MI: Revell, 2009), 20.

night filled with passion and excitement.

Pulling up to the hotel, Amanda was raring to go! Then. . . Nathan, her groom, couldn't find his wallet. He instructed his new bride to go up to the room and *get ready*. What?! Amanda *was* ready! She just needed her groom, but he was obsessed with finding his wallet.

When Amanda got to their room—alone—she first had a cry then fixed her makeup, perfumed herself, and lay on the bed looking as sexy as she could. Then, she waited. . .and waited. . .and waited. No groom. She waited some more. . . until finally she had had enough waiting. Still in her wedding dress, she went downstairs. Amanda found her groom— *who was supposed to be exploring her!*—tearing apart his truck looking for his wallet.

Amanda went back to their room, took off her wedding dress, and had a feast on the food she had saved from their reception. The next morning, they drove to Nathan's parents' house. He had left his wallet in his tux pants pocket. Then they drove eight hours to their honeymoon destination.

Nathan, not realizing her desire for him to undress her while she was still in her wedding dress, unknowingly complained about dragging said dress around. Amanda snapped after he referred to it as her "dumb dress" and told him she had hoped he would have taken off her "dumb dress" as part of the passionate night she had mapped out in her mind. Poor Nathan didn't have a clue.[2]

Groom, please don't allow anything to get in the way of

---

2 Marla Taviano, *Is That All He Thinks About?* (Eugene, OR: Harvest House Publishers, 2007), 117–18.

your first night together. Focus completely on her.

We've all heard these horror stories. Some of us have lived them. I've heard of brides and grooms who locked themselves in the bathroom the night of their wedding and refused to come out. Yes, men have done this, too! There's quite a bit that can and will go wrong on that highly anticipated night.

I don't want to leave you with only horror stories. Many couples have spectacular experiences. You don't hear about those as much because most want to keep those intimate moments private, and rightly so. However, I've heard of many who had a plan, took their time, and slowly uncovered God's special wedding gift for the bride and groom. Few adventures will ever compare, and then you experience the grand finale of waking up to your best friend every day for the rest of your life. It's like a fun slumber party with your friends, only better!

Having said that, it's normal to be a bit scared or maybe a little uncertain. And it's okay to be excited and eager for that first encounter, too.

You ladies may be asking yourself, *Is it okay to be sexy, sensual, and alluring for my husband?* Or you might be thinking, *I've stifled that part of me for so long, to remain within the boundaries of God's commands, I don't know if I can switch it over.*

To answer the first question, "'Awake, O north wind, and come, wind of the south; make my garden breathe out fragrance, let its spices be wafted abroad. May my beloved come into his garden and eat its choice fruits!'" (Song of Solomon 4:16). That sounds pretty sensual to me—that would be YES.

The latter question is a bit more complicated and one we

will address more thoroughly as we go, but it starts with a change in your mindset. You've been telling yourself, *No, no, no, chill out. Whoa there, Nelly!* But now it's time (once you're officially married) to change that to, *Let 'er rip! Send in the horses! Blow the horn!*

## Get Acquainted with Your Anatomy

Guys, you can glance over this section; this is for the ladies.

It's time to get acquainted with your anatomy. Trust me, he knows his! No joke, since the time he was five (give or take a couple of years) he became very aware of how his body worked, and he had no problem discovering just how the tide rolled in. Ask any mother of a little boy and she will tell you they are all about self-discovery; and not only that, but they think it's the best thing since Hot Wheels.

Hopefully, he had a mother who didn't put him down in this area. One of my boys during potty training used to call his penis a "peedee" (because that was where his urine came from). Adorable! We did tell him the correct name was "penis," but he still insisted on the name *he* gave it. One day he proudly announced to me, "Mom, I got a big peedee!" Not wanting him to have any negative input about his favorite appendage, I replied, "Yes, you sure do."

Take time to look at yourself in the way your future husband will look at you. Not as flawed, *Oh, I hate this part, and I can't stand that part,* focusing on the bumps and lumps of your body. Instead take in the beauty of what God made. That's right! God made your body with all of its imperfections, and it *is* beautiful.

Imagine what Adam saw the first time his eyes saw Eve (Genesis 2:23). Imagine what Adam was thinking. Imagine his excitement when he realized Eve was all his. She was all his to explore and all his to enjoy. Whoa! That is exactly how your husband will feel when he sees you! He will *not* be looking at the bumps and lumps. You can trust me on this one!

Give yourself grace and give him grace, too.

And, men (*welcome back, men!*), don't ever stop telling her how beautiful she looks to you. She will never get tired of hearing it!

## Talk about Your Expectations

Most likely your aim, for your first night together, is to hit a hole in one with mind-blowing sex. I applaud your enthusiasm. What guy doesn't want to hit a hole in one? However, at the end of round one, the only thing blown will probably be your unrealistic expectations, leaving you disappointed. The cure for this is to change your target. Instead, aim for a night of discovery. A night to enjoy each other's bodies and the incredible way God has designed us for sex. You can still hit the mark, even if the sex isn't "mind-blowing," as long as you change the target.

## Don't Expect Him to Be like What You've Seen in a Movie

He may be a bit awkward. Don't expect him to be like the latest movie star voted the Sexiest Man Alive! And, men, don't expect her to act like an exotic dancer. What you've seen in TV shows and the movies IS NOT REAL! There are cameras and other people around. The director looking for the best shot shouts, "Cut! Let's do that again!" The *sexy* actor knows exactly what to do because it's all in the script and the director is *directing* him. In this show, *you* get to be the director.

Men, she may not like *everything* you do. In every fictitious scene you've watched on TV and in movies, the woman loves *everything* her man does. And she never turns him down regardless of what bizarre thing he wants to do. Your wife may jump because you accidentally tickled her or cringe because she feels an unexpected sensation. She is not rejecting you! It will take time for her to get into her sexual stride. Be patient with her.

The truth is, most men really don't know what to do to please their women. Discover your rhythm as a couple. Dr. Kevin Leman warns brides-to-be not to expect a groom to be knowledgeable, even if it's not his first time. "A what?" is the response from many men when Dr. Leman asked if they knew what a clitoris was.[3]

Ladies, you may think he will always know what to do. Think about that for a minute. He will need to learn you and what you like and don't like. Decide ahead of time that you will approach your intimacy with an eagerness to learn and please. You'll both want to hit it over the fence, but sex is a team sport. You will hit many home runs over the years, but in order to do that you'll need to cooperate and communicate. . .and practice.

---

3 Leman, *Under the Sheets*, 20.

## Cooperate and Communicate

Good cooperation takes a lot of communication. I know when it gets to this special night, you will want to play ball and not communicate. But let's take a time-out. The healthiest marriages are the ones in which the two involved are best friends. Best friends who get to be naked and explore each other's bodies. You get to enjoy each other physically and passionately. And best friends talk about everything. Trust and great sex are closely related. As a couple, good healthy communication is what will sustain you when you can't pay your rent, when his mom keeps calling at the worst times, when he loses his job, and when the kids keep pounding on your door interrupting that perfect moment.

Spend some time talking about what you both expect for your first time together. This advice comes with a warning. As you talk about sex, be extremely careful. You may need to have this conversation over the phone or *after* the pastor pronounces you Mr. and Mrs. Happy-for-life. You don't want to be lured into being too physical and blow it at the last minute. You've waited this long. Don't sink the spectacular voyage that awaits you.

Talk about your fears. Talk about your expectations. Talk about desiring him to carry you into your bedroom suite. Talk about wanting her to praise your every move. You are going to be husband and wife and live together for fifty-plus years. Start your life together with good communication in all subjects but especially with your sexual relationship.

## Be Realistic

Be realistic. Don't have unreasonable expectations. Ladies, you may be secretly thinking or hoping that you'll have (like the magazines tout) multiple orgasms. Is it possible? Yes. Is it probable? Ahh...no.

Listen: You'll be lucky to have *one* on your first night. Be prepared that it may not happen on the first round. But so what! That's not unusual. You've got your whole life to work at this!

And, men, you may be thinking that you'll be able to go multiple rounds (if you know what I mean), but perhaps one time will be more realistic. It's the connection that matters, not the number of times you connect.

Consider the first few times as batting practice. If you hit it over the fence, terrific! But it can still be great even if you don't come anywhere near the fence. What's important to remember is that this is only the beginning of a long sexual life *together*. You have your whole married life to figure this out. Don't expect to cover it all in just one night.

Think of Christopher Columbus. Be a voyager. Explore each other's bodies. Figure it out together. Team sport, remember?

Have fun! Laugh even. Yes. Laugh. Together. It's okay to laugh together. You don't have to be super serious. Your bedroom should be the most fun room in the house. (After you're married, of course!)

A special note to the ladies: never, never, never laugh *at him*. And take your time and relax. If you're tense, it will not go well. If you do feel tense or can't seem to relax, then tell him. Ask him to slow down if you need him to. Like Momma said when you were two, "Use your words." Keep in mind he has been holding back for a long time. He may be ready to sprint, but you may need to jog for a while.

Typically, it takes some time for women to warm up for sex. Men, on the other hand, tend to be ready to go with just a look, an unclasped button, or the words "Let's go."

Tommy Nelson explains how men and women tend to have very different gauges regarding appropriate sexual behavior, exemplified in the following wedding night story about a guy he knew in college. This groom scared his new wife silly on their wedding night by coming at her with unbridled thirst. She had no previous sexual experience and was very nervous about their first time together. He, having played out every fantasy a guy could think of in his mind—and raring to go to play each one out on their first night—emerged from their hotel bathroom like "Conan the Barbarian." He then proceeded to pour out every bit of passion he had on her and, in his words, "scared her to death!" Thereafter, she needed years of counseling before she could begin to accept her sexuality and embrace him with any passion.[4]

One thing you definitely want to avoid on your first night is a terrifying experience requiring years of counseling. Communication is the key.

---

4 Tommy Nelson, *The Book of Romance* (Nashville, TN: Thomas Nelson, 2007), 95.

## Getting Her Ready for Conan

Men, you may be thinking, *How will I know when she's ready?* Ladies, you might be thinking the same thing. Or you may be wondering, *What about the hymen?* You may be apprehensive and a bit hesitant with concerns that it will hurt. Men, clearly the last thing you want is for her to experience pain. These are all normal thoughts but nothing to be anxious about.

The vagina is self-lubricating. It will naturally prepare itself for Mr. Excited. This is nothing to worry about. Relax and enjoy being close and able to "touch" after being husband and wife. As a backup, it's probably not a bad idea to purchase some lubricant. (Yes, you can buy that stuff! Get it online if you're too embarrassed to walk into a store.) Some couples find this critical, while others don't need it at all. Be prepared for both scenarios.

Another section for the ladies: if your hymen hasn't already been broken—and if you are a virgin, it most likely hasn't—then your first sexual experience could be a bit painful. In some rare cases, the hymen can be broken from playing sports or activities, such as riding a horse.

How painful? If you've ever had anything pierced, like your ears or. . .(*ahem*). . .other body parts, then it's definitely not more painful than that. It may not even be painful at all. If it's a concern, you might want to start with you on top of your prince so you can control the pressure. Then after the initial takeoff, when the captain announces you're free to move around the aircraft, you can change it up. There probably will be some blood when your hymen breaks. And in rare cases you could have a little bleeding for a few weeks after each time you have intercourse as well. This is nothing to be alarmed about. If it persists for several weeks, contact your doctor.

If for some reason you're still experiencing pain after the initial break of the hymen, this is where the lubricant becomes your best friend. Don't be afraid to use it. Don't be timid in asking him to slow down, change positions, or to stop so you can grab your lubricant. (You'll be glad you kept it close.) And don't be surprised if Mr. Excited slips off course. You didn't do anything wrong. Just help direct him back on track. Don't expect to be a sexual dynamo right out of the virgin gate. It will most likely take time for you to ease into this title. If by chance you are able to reach dynamo ranking quickly, good for you, go buy yourself a medal! This, however, is very unlikely. Allow yourself time to build to such an award-winning classification. You'll get there eventually if you work at it.

## Dealing with Painful Intercourse Together

In the event she continues to have pain during intercourse, there are some things you can try. It might help if Mr. Excited goes very slowly and moves inch by inch. He may want to imitate a jackhammer, but she might be more up for the horse on the merry-go-round that slowly goes up and down. Simply let him know, and when her body becomes more familiar with this new activity, she'll soon be ready for more variety. Think about what's happening: this area of her body has not had any action and now suddenly aggressive repeated friction is occurring.

As you both learn to relax and go with the flow, it will get much better. But until then, you can also try extending your foreplay so she can loosen up. He most likely won't need that; however, most ladies probably will. Direct him to areas you'd like to be touched that will relax and stimulate you. You'll have to discover this *together*. The longer the foreplay, the better her body can prepare for Mr. Excited. Another thing you may want to try is for her to reach orgasm before intercourse. (Figure it out. . .*together*.) This can relax her and give her a chance to "indulge" more fully.

The main purpose is to enjoy each other completely.

Chances are it will go pretty quick. Sustained performance is something most couples learn with time. However, if you're experiencing painful intercourse on a regular basis, consult your physician. Before you do, you can try taking a couple of days off to see if it helps for your body to rest and recover a bit. This doesn't mean you have to stop "having fun"; there's a lot you can do besides intercourse.

As in all things in marriage, communication is key. Learn to be flexible.

This brings me to another point I want to cover—PE, premature ejaculation, also known as rapid ejaculation. Unfortunately, more and more couples have to deal with this, and it's best to be informed and prepared. It's not necessary to be overconcerned; however, don't create a problem where you might not have one. Accept this as only information, and tuck it away in your preparing-for-marriage file.

In *He's Just Not Up for It Anymore*, authors Bob Berkowitz,

PhD, and Susan Yager-Berkowitz explain that premature ejaculation is a reason some men avoid sexual intimacy with their partners. PE sufferers usually have no control over this unwanted but universal complaint leaving men with feelings of "inadequacy and shame." With 25 percent of American men suffering from PE, it's more common than many people realize. PE can be defined as when ejaculation happens before insertion or in less than one minute after. It's no wonder these men oftentimes prefer rolling solo rather than to face the embarrassment PE can bring.[5]

If PE happens and he doesn't quite make it the first time, don't despair. Ladies, instead consider it a compliment. This is something—as you both progress—in your sexual relationship you can attack together. (*In a fun way!*) Let him know you'll go for it again in an hour (*or maybe less*) or in the morning. Relax! You have all night to enjoy each other. Don't do anything that will cause him to feel bad, and obviously do not tease him about it. Make sure you let him know it's okay and you're happy doing countless other things to bring you both pleasure. Sound okay, men?

If it does become an issue, you can discuss and work through it together. One of the purposes of sex, by God's design, is mutual satisfaction. It bonds a couple, but it also debuts as a time to fully enjoy each other. If one or both of you feels unsatisfied, this becomes a serious issue in a marriage and one you must address. Decide beforehand that if either of you struggles in this area, you will tackle it together and make your "fun time" a top priority. This

5 Bob Berkowitz, PhD, and Susan Yager-Berkowitz, *He's Just Not Up for It Anymore* (New York: HarperCollins, 2009), 141.

would definitely be a *WE* problem.

Once again, cooperation and communication is crucial. Have a plan knowing how you'll respond, and make sure you are gracious and accommodating.

If one of you is "ready" before the other (most likely him), there is plenty you can do to keep *everyone* happy until you are *both* ready. Don't fret; take a little more time. Be Christopher Columbus.

Most of all, keep in mind you are joined together in marriage. Two become one. Remember 1 Corinthians 7:4, about our spouse having authority over our body? In other words, take responsibility for each other's enjoyment.

## Enjoy and Have Fun

Above all, enjoy each other. Be tender and understanding, discovering what each of you enjoys together. Express delight and appreciation for each other. Go all out! Enjoy! Soak each other in! Give it your all. And don't stop until Jesus comes back! It's okay after you're married.

Enjoy his masculinity. Enjoy her beauty. Enjoy his strength. Enjoy her femininity. Enjoy his ability to be completely focused. Don't expect her to have the ability to be as "focused" as you. When he comes at you in a way that seems strange or you see him naked for the first time, don't tense up or withdraw. When you ask yourself, "*Why did she do that?*" or "*What is he doing?*" remember your bodies are formed completely different, and what brings one of you pleasure may do little for the other.

Both men and women can be very sensitive when it comes to sex. You may think that sex for him is carefree, nonchalant, blasé, or even jocular. This is not the case at all. Sex is very important to most men. Sex is a delicate matter for him. Men, don't you agree? Open up and talk about this.

Ladies, listen up! You do not—I repeat, *you do not*—want to do or say *anything* that could cause him to feel inadequate. Not in the area of lovemaking nor in any area. Do not make sexual jokes at his expense. A joke to you could be very hurtful to him. Are you listening? Do not play around with this. His penis means a great deal to him. To him, it's like a Purple Heart, an Olympic gold medal, and a Super Bowl ring all rolled into one. Never, never, never say anything negative about it—*ever*. Only say words of praise and adoration. This is no laughing matter. Stay focused, and really hear this.

One lady told me that after she and her significant other were done making love, she said, "Is that it?" Another woman told me that after her first time, she asked him, "Were you all the way in?" Ouch! Use your brain, ladies. Don't say such things. Words like this could devastate a man. Make sure "Eww," "Yuck," or "Gross" never pass from your lips. Ever!

Men, always be gentle with her, and don't be afraid to ask her what she likes. This is not the time to act like Tarzan or a caveman; let your soft and sensitive side out, and she will respond to Mr. Sensitive more.

Afterward, ladies, make sure you go into the bathroom and urinate. Seriously. You can get an extremely painful infection if you don't. It's not uncommon for a newlywed to get a urinary tract infection, Honeymoon Cystitis, due to underestimating the necessity of urinating after intercourse. Make sure you empty your bladder *every time* and as soon as possible. But in the event you are one of those learn-the-hard-way gals and think you can ignore this warning, these are the symptoms: pain or burning during urination and/or the feeling you have to urinate often but when you do very little comes out. Lower belly pain. Cloudy and/or smelly urine. In more severe cases, there can be back pain and/or blood in the urine as well. Be smart. Empty your bladder, ladies.

When you arrive back from the bathroom, don't be surprised if you find your shining knight sound asleep. Don't be offended but instead consider this, too, a compliment—he poured all of his love and affection on you, and now he is wiped out. You can tell yourself what a good lover you are and that you are the ultimate of women. But before you go too far in patting yourself on the back, know there is a medical reason for this. In *Intimate Issues*, authors Linda Dillow and Lorraine Pintus write: "During sex, a man's body releases oxytocin, a hormone thought to cause drowsiness, which makes him want to sleep."[6]

Oxytocin is also known as the bonding hormone. This will bond you as a couple. As usual, God thought of everything! It's like a superglue-bond.

If he does doze off after, just curl up next to him and thank God for a man who loves you and gives you his all. Men, you may need to be told that most women like to cuddle after sex. Ladies, don't forget to tell him how AMAZING he was and

---

6 Linda Dillow and Lorraine Pintus, *Intimate Issues* (Colorado Springs, CO: WaterBrook Publishing, 2000), 40.

what you liked. The information will come in handy for the next round.

Never stop telling each other how much you enjoy your "fun." Ladies, always communicate how much you appreciate him as a lover, and praise him often. Men, never stop telling her how beautiful she is and how much you love her. Yes, say "I love you" often. Always express your delight of each other physically and otherwise.

Ladies, when you like something, *tell him*. Build him up, show admiration, express delight, and give your approval, and he will feel like Conan. People will wonder why he's smiling all the time, but you will *know* why he's smiling all the time.

Men, treat her like a princess and she will improve with age. Protect her, be soft with her, be patient with her, and cherish her. Every woman yearns to be cherished. And all the women said, "Amen!"

Decide to be fully and 100 percent committed to your marriage. On a daily basis, choose to love, honor, respect, and cherish each other. Never forget—out of the billions of people in this world, *you* chose your beloved. Decide *before* you get married that you will treat your spouse so well that each day he/she is thanking God for you. Every day give him or her reason to say, "I won the lotto in love!" Ladies, do this and you will truly have your knight in shining armor. Men, do this and you will always have a princess worthy of praise.

# Discussion Questions

- What are your expectations for your first "big night"? Discuss any fears or expectations.

- Was sex something discussed in your home? What did your parents teach you or not teach you about sex?

- How often do you want to have sex after you're married?

- Are there any experiences from your past that might hinder your sexual enjoyment?

- How will you handle when one of you wants to be intimate but the other does not?

# Chapter Ten
## Keeping the Bedroom Steamy

Waiting until their wedding night to have sex, Charlie and Janessa were sizzling and ready to go. The long-awaited night couldn't have been any more perfect in their romantic honeymoon suite—candles, a beautiful view, flowers—all with a Jacuzzi tub in the center of their room. Still in their wedding attire they entered their room with eager anticipation. As the room became "steamy," Charlie turned on the water for the hot tub while he was helping Janessa out of her wedding dress, doing his best to keep things "moving along" with kisses and passion. Things were *really* steaming up!

Then *the unfortunate incident* occurred. Charlie reached down to [dramatic pause] turn on the jets for the hot tub [dramatic pause], but the jetting water came shooting out of the tub, and [dramatic pause], with full force, hit Janessa square in the face!

They both erupted with hysterical laughter. Not at all what they had anticipated, nonetheless, they turned what could have been a disaster into fun. "It was probably the best thing for our sex life," Janessa explained. "We learned immediately that it's okay to laugh and have fun!" And they haven't stopped "having fun" since.

Have fun! I said this in chapter nine, and it's worth repeating: *your bedroom needs to be the most fun room in the house.* God designed sex for your enjoyment as a couple, and for fun, laughter, connectedness, and wholeness—cementing you like nothing else can, uniting you as a couple.

What if unlike Charlie and Janessa, you've already been "united" as a couple and your wedding night will not be your first sexual experience together? The last thing I want for you would be to enter into your marriage with any guilt or shame. You probably started out with the utmost intentions to do the physical stuff God's way, and you didn't realize how difficult it would be.

Sex is very powerful, and romantic relationships lead to sexual intimacy; this was God's design. It starts with the first time you hold hands, and then it feels like every molecule in the universe pulls you together. . .until you've gone too far. If this is you, make amends with God, *and* with each other. Read Psalm 51. Take particular notice of verse 7, "Purify me with hyssop, and I shall be clean; wash me, and I shall be whiter than snow."

Even King David, who the Bible describes as being "a man after My [God's] heart, who will do all My will" (Acts 13:22), struggled with sexual sin, and God greatly used him. If you're not married yet, you can start over and wait until you're married. Either way, your story is not over. You can get right with God today.

If you've held your ground against *every molecule in the universe* and are waiting until marriage, I encourage you to make it to the finish line. I guarantee it will be worth it. For those of you chanting, "It's not possible. It's not possible—" oh contraire, yes it is. I know many couples who crossed this finish line with flying colors. You can do the same.

Keep in mind, sex was not designed for selfishness. The target is mutual satisfaction and fulfillment. In her book *Kiss Me Again*, Barbara Wilson writes: "When we make intimacy, not pleasure, the primary goal of sex, everyone wins. Because pleasure is the natural outcome when we pursue true intimacy."[1]

God created sex, and our first stop needs to be looking into the Bible about this. Don't you agree?

Sex is not to be used as a weapon, nor withheld for selfish reasons: "Stop depriving one another, except by agreement for a time, so that you may devote yourselves to prayer, and come together again so that Satan will not temp you because of your lack of self-control" (1 Corinthians 7:5).

Don't leave your spouse to be tempted by Satan! You want to make sure your beloved is fully armed for whatever schemes or trickery the evil one has brewing. Never send him or her out into the world "wanting."

I love the way author Elisabeth Elliot speaks of her first husband, who had been killed on the mission field, when she explains how Jim Elliot said that we are to live to the fullest in everything, which is the will of God. She adds that in the area of their sexual relationship he fully committed to this mantra. Elliot declares, "God intends for you to abandon yourself and enjoy it [sex]."[2]

1 Barbara Wilson, *Kiss Me Again* (Colorado Springs, CO: Multnomah, 2009), 150.
2 Elliot, *The Mark of a Man*, 162.

One common dilemma I hear from Christian people is: "I'm not sure what God's will is for my life." Certainly the mark of a sincere follower of Jesus Christ is the active search and pursuit of the will of God. But oftentimes we tend to complicate this and ignore the obvious.

Please hear this: If you are married, it is God's will that you have a fulfilled and vibrant sex life. Pause for a minute and let that sink in. He created our bodies with this very purpose in mind. Not convinced? Let's see what God has to say on this subject, shall we?

*Let your fountain be blessed, and rejoice in the wife of your youth. As a loving hind and a graceful doe, let her breasts satisfy you at all times; be exhilarated always with her love.*

—PROVERBS 5:18–19

*"He has brought me to his banquet hall, and his banner over me is love. Sustain me with raisin cakes, refresh me with apples, because I am lovesick. Let his left hand be under my head and his right hand embrace me."*

—SONG OF SOLOMON 2:4–6

*"I have come into my garden, my sister, my bride; I have gathered my myrrh along with my balsam. I have eaten my honeycomb and my honey; I have drunk my wine and my milk. Eat, friends; drink and imbibe deeply, O lovers."*

—SONG OF SOLOMON 5:1

Talk about sensuous and erotic desire!

And speaking of erotic, some of you may be thinking, *What's okay and acceptable in the bedroom? Is oral sex okay? What about sex toys?*

Frankly, the Bible doesn't explicitly say what is acceptable and what is not, only that sex is strictly for marriage.

## Let's Talk about This

The speaker was a lovely woman and bravely took on the subject of sex at one of the sessions during a women's retreat. Have you ever noticed in the church we talk a lot about sex *before* a couple is married, and less after? You go from *no* to *go* after a long-awaited ceremony and celebration. Some enter marriage wondering what's okay or struggle with ideologies of what's acceptable and godly. In this particular retreat session there were many soon-to-be-wed young ladies. During the question-and-answer time, one darling young woman raised her hand. Timidly she softly and hesitantly asked, "Is oral sex okay?" Silence. Adding to the silence and the awkwardness, which now consumed the room, was the look of shock on the speaker's face. Think deer in headlights. My heart went out to this poor *dear*, as well as the young lady who asked the question. The speaker then did a nice dodge, leaving the question unanswered.

After the session was over, the ladies turned to *me*. Frankly, sex is not an easy subject for me either, but because I believe it's such a vital part of marriage I'll talk about it, when asked. (And when not asked sometimes, too.) In light of this, I was happy to talk with the ladies.

You can search the whole Bible and you will not find any precise instructions regarding what is, and is not, okay with regard to married sex. I think God did this on purpose, leaving it up to each individual couple.

Are there certain things you want to do? If it's okay with him, if it's okay with her, then it's okay. For instance, many *godly* couples use what one could call—*ahem*—sex toys, to enhance their time together. Is it wrong? You will need to decide.

As soon as one of you feels uncomfortable with the idea of "further exploration," it's time for pause. If you're the one saying no to "exploration," ask yourself why. If you want to try something but your spouse doesn't, don't push. Wait patiently and ask him/her to pray about it. If any activity causes physical or emotional harm to your spouse, this would be a clear no. Be sensitive and understanding.

However, scripture does give us some clues:

- "...and his fruit was sweet to my taste" (Song of Solomon 2:3).
- "...and eat its choice fruits!" (Song of Solomon 4:16).
- "...I have eaten my honeycomb and my honey..." (Song of Solomon 5:1).
- "...Eat, friends..." (Song of Solomon 5:1).
- "Your stature is like a palm tree, and your breasts are like its clusters. I said, 'I will climb the palm tree, I will take hold of its fruit stalks.' Oh, may your breasts

be like clusters of the vine, and the fragrance of your
breath like apples, and your mouth like the best
wine!" (Song of Solomon 7:7–9).

Some may argue these are merely symbols, but you can't
deny God's choice in words, so you decide. These descriptive
words give suggestion for exploration, for sure! Pleasure, in-
dulgence, and unity are undeniable themes.

Some struggle with the notion of one being sexual *and*
godly. Read through the Song of Solomon, and then tell me
sexual and godly don't go together. I really can't stress this
enough. God intends for you to completely embrace. . .go all
out. . .and totally enjoy your spouse *physically*.

Now, I am going to elaborate more on something we've
glanced over several times, because, gentlemen, I really want
you to get this. The Bible gives you another huge clue in becoming the Don Juan of the love garden:

- "How beautiful you are, my darling, how beautiful
  you are! Your eyes are like doves" (Song of Solomon
  1:15).
- "How beautiful you are, my darling, how beautiful
  you are! Your eyes are like doves behind your veil;
  your hair is like a flock of goats that have descended
  from Mount Gilead" (Song of Solomon 4:1).
- "You are altogether beautiful, my darling, and there
  is no blemish in you" (Song of Solomon 4:7).
- "You are as beautiful as Tirzah, my darling, as lovely
  as Jerusalem, as awesome as an army with banners"

(Song of Solomon 6:4).
- "The curves of your hips are like jewels" (Song of Solomon 7:1).
- "How beautiful and how delightful you are, my love, with all your charms!" (Song of Solomon 7:6).

To spell it out: Tell her she's beautiful and how appealing she looks to you *often*. Especially when she is unclothed. The more you express your delight for her and her body, the more she will feel comfortable in her birthday suit. Many women feel insecure about how they look. When a man can fully communicate his feelings about his wife's form and beauty, it will tremendously resonate with her, and she will be more apt to show it to you. Get it? Many times the imperfections we women see in our bodies are the very parts our men love the most. I strongly dislike that my stomach isn't as flat as I want it to be, and my husband *loves* that it's not as flat as I want it to be. Go figure.

Never stop telling her how beautiful she is to you. Even thirty, forty, or more years into your marriage, *keep telling her*.

These scriptures also give us a clue for the ladies, too—*what he sees matters greatly to your man*. Men are visual. God created men this way, so use this to enhance your intimate time together. Entice him by keeping *his eyes* enticed. Be proud to flaunt your stuff for your man. (When you're alone, of course!)

As a general rule, women tend to be more emotional. She needs to know you care and *feel* connected, before she wants to be "connected" to you. Check in with her regularly, plug in emotionally and spiritually, and then sit back and see how *physical* she is with you.

## Pray Together

Praying together will unite you in a way that is indescribable—words such as *electric, fire,* and *steamy* would definitely apply. If you really want to ramp up your sex life, ramp up your prayer life, and pray together.

## Keeping WE Strong

Sexual intimacy needs to be a priority in your marriage. Write in, "connecting" at the top of your schedule. Do you want to safeguard your marriage? Sex can be one of the strongest safeguards. When you expect to be "intimate" on a regular basis, it will force you to always be in harmony. If you were to get out of sync, angry, irked, or bothered by your spouse, getting naked is the last thing you'll want to do. But if you work on being in harmony and *ready for action*, it forces you to always work on your relationship. What's happening in the "romance department" will give you a pretty good gauge on the overall health of your marriage. Have a mutual understanding that you will have sex on a regular basis, making it a matter of *when*, not *if.*

Most men feel like they are cutting themselves open with vulnerability when they request sex. Ladies, don't dismiss this lightly; a denial can leave him wounded in ways most women do not understand. Which is why in chapter seven I advised alternative suggestions to saying no. Do you remember what they were? *Can it be quick?* (As in, *I've got to get to work, but I have fifteen minutes.*) *Later? Tomorrow?*

News flash: *Now* is always the best answer. But if you have to say no—guys, too—make a date for another time.

I was speaking at a women's conference, and during a question-and-answer session, somehow the room got on a tangent about when it was okay to turn down a request from your husband for sex. The excuses started flying from "time-of-the-month," or "fatigue," to "frustrated and overworked."

I sat quietly listening to the many excuses. Numerous women were jumping in, encouraging one another with "good reasons to say no." When I'd heard enough and had a pretty good pulse on the room, as gently as I could I addressed the no-to-sex avalanche.

"Ladies, please, we can come up with a million reasons to say no. But *WHY* in the world would you want to? You are the only one your husband can go to for his sexual needs. It's not as if he can go next door. And I'm sure you wouldn't want him to. Think of it this way, he is running the marathon of life and *you* are the only one with the life-sustaining water he needs. Why in the world would you deny him? If he were running a marathon and you had a cup of water for him, how mean would it be of you to pour it on the ground? When you withhold sex from him, this is essentially what you are doing to the man you chose and promised to love and honor. You, and only you, hold the cup of water he needs."

The room went silent.

from me to we

During another speaking engagement with both men and women, I said something receiving a reaction, which, frankly, surprised me. I wish I could have taken a picture, because I have never seen so many jaws drop at once, from men and women alike. Are you curious what I said?

My husband and I had been given a relatively short amount of time to talk on the subject of sex. I had grappled intensely over what to say in such a short time. "In our home," getting right to the point, "the policy is, *the store is always open.*" Shock rippled through the room. I sincerely did not expect such a reaction—to something I believe needs to be commonplace—especially in Christian homes.

Ladies, your man may strike out at work, hit a foul with a new venture, dribble on the investment field—*but in the bedroom* he needs to always hit a home run!

Don't just take my word for it. Dr. Kevin Leman says sex is the great equalizer for a man and that it energizes him, builds his confidence, and boosts his overall sense of well-being. When a man has a willing wife waiting for him at home, he can feel fulfilled even if his job is unfulfilling—she gives him the strength to keep going. In addition, this gives him purpose as he works toward his reward at the end of a long day.

Sex cures all kinds of ailments for a man: from illnesses to problems at work, money struggles, and even marriage problems. Even if he acts like "a four-year-old who shaves," if you are the woman whom this man comes home to—and can't get enough of—you are one fortunate woman![3]

---

3 Leman, *Under the Sheets*, 91.

## When He Bunts

What about when *he* says no? This is a much more complicated issue to address. But first, think back to chapter seven,
and not acting like his mother. Many times when a relationship has gotten to a point where a man is refusing sex with
his wife, it can possibly be due to one pivotal reason. Here
it is in a nutshell: withholding sexual intimacy is his last at-
tempt to gain control. Which is why I caution you to fully
grasp chapter seven and heed the recommendations given.

There are, of course, other reasons as well. As a man ages,
his body changes, along with testosterone levels and how
"Mr. Excited" functions.

Impotence can happen for various reasons, such as health
issues or the use of medications, most of which are most
likely temporary. Good communication can help you fish out
what the reason is. Having said this, sometimes "Mr. Excited"
just doesn't want to cooperate. The cause could be stress,
tiredness, nervousness, temporary illness, anxiety, depression,
alcohol use, to name a few—these culprits can lead men to
experience unpredictable and unwanted challenges. We don't
hear about this, because what man announces "difficulty" or
talks about it over coffee with friends? They'd sooner have a
molar pulled!

On the other hand, if a man never says no, one reason
could be he's starved—in other words, his sexual desires are
not being filled. Most men say no at some point, and more
specifically, those who are "filled." Ladies, never take this
personally but instead as a compliment. Him saying no can
mean his sexual desires are being met, or you're catching him

at a highly stressful time, or he's physically exhausted. Be understanding, and don't make it about *you*. And whatever you do, don't create your own sad tale questioning if you're pretty enough, or if he loves you, or if he finds you attractive. This is highly unfruitful and a total waste of brain cells. Make an appointment with him for another time. And. Move. On.

If he's always saying no, then you have a serious problem and one that needs to be addressed—lovingly. If the reason is because he's experiencing the inability to maintain an erection, see a doctor; there are many forms of treatment, plus, a checkup would be in order.

## Connect

Reciprocally enjoy each other. To be fully sexually fulfilled, mutual satisfaction stands as your goal. If either of you are not having fun, the experience will not be all it's supposed to be. No one wants to play tennis with an unenthusiastic partner! If you're complying because you feel it's your duty to do so, you've arrived at the wrong concept. Instead, *savor*, *relish*, and *delight in* are better images. Showing delight for another person is very powerful—in fact, it's one of the most powerful things you can do, whether inside or outside of the bedroom.

Ladies, we've talked a lot about how important sex is for a man; know that it is just as important for you, too. Hear this: There is nothing better than starting your day feeling loved, cherished, connected, and appreciated. For both of you! His appetite for you will not be amply satisfied unless *you* are satisfied. He receives his enjoyment from your enjoyment. It matters greatly to him that you are an active participant and that you are pleased with your "activities." Just ask him.

Communication is key. If at any point in your relationship you stop having sex, you need to talk about it. Start with good communication about this subject right from the start. It amazes me how many couples will "get naked" together but won't talk about "getting naked" together. Talk. Communicate. Share your desires and needs.

When we have open dialogue with vulnerable communication—sharing who we really are—it will lead to lasting trust. The ability to fully trust will have huge implications in your sex life. The measure in which you are able to do this will also measure your enjoyment of each other during your sexual escapades. When you completely trust another person, you let go and freely give *all of yourself.* Establishing trust in the everyday—in what can seem mundane—leads to ecstasy in the bedroom. That's right, those couples who are polite, cordial, considerate, respectful, and courteous toward each other are most likely the ones having the most fun behind closed doors. How you treat your spouse "off of the playing field" will have huge implications "on the playing field."

Sex and trust are bed partners.

What goes into building solid trust?

Feelings—Being able to trust another with our feelings and feeling safe has huge implications for intimacy. Feelings may lie to us from time to time, but it's never wrong to acknowledge those feelings and deal with them. Talk through feelings with your loved one, and be a safe place for each other to land.

Reliability—Being reliable can be defined as doing what you say you're going to do. Waiting for someone who doesn't show up or shows up extremely late slowly erodes trust. It's hurtful to do to another person, and over time that person becomes unsafe to us. If you told her you'd take her to her favorite pizza place for dinner but came home too late to do so, she's going to have a difficult time "warming up" to you. If he was counting on you for a task that was important to him, letting him down weakens his trust for you. Show up for each other when you're being counted on. Be sure to keep your promises.

Apology—When we've wronged our spouse, we need to own it and apologize. It's very difficult to trust a person who never apologizes or doesn't take responsibility for his or her actions.

Open Communication—Being able to talk through issues and, more importantly, resolve those issues will have big payoffs in the "fun zone." Keep this a priority.

Honesty—Does this really need an explanation? No one trusts someone who lies.

Honor—Couples who continually show honor will continually have the most "fun." Think of ways to honor your spouse daily with encouraging words, acts of kindness, listening, supporting, and being present. This means putting away your cell phone or any other electronic device and giving him/her your full attention.

Other-centeredness—Looking out for your beloved—and not merely thinking of yourself—putting *WE* before

*ME* will enhance your entire relationship. This will be like a tiny seed growing into a mighty, strong, veracious oak tree that keeps growing—the more you consider your spouse, the more consideration you will receive. *And the more affection you will receive!* A person who looks out for another is easy to trust.

Confidence—Keep secrets. Use discretion. Always be kind. This sounds oversimplified, I know, but when the busyness of life happens, many forget to practice these essential and simple courtesies. Keep your relationship free from any doubt regarding faithfulness and love.

What happens in the bedroom *stays* in the bedroom. She will not feel safe if you share your "private encounters" with your buddies. He will feel betrayed if he overhears you talking to your mom or a girlfriend about his "moves." What you choose to do as a couple is private and needs to remain strictly between the two of you, only. Keep your private time just that, *private.*

## Keeping Love Steamy

How you treat each other throughout the day can be a natural and easy progression to sexual expression. On days when you have to part, always send the other off with sweet kisses and hugs. At the end of the day, greet your spouse warmly, like he or she is the most important person in the world! After all, he/she is, right? I always feel sad when I see couples reunite at the end of the day with little more than a casual hello, as if they were merely the barista serving him/her coffee.

This is your king coming home. This is your queen. Show enthusiasm.

My heart still jumps when I see my husband's car pulling into our driveway. If you were to watch my house, you'd see me rushing out to greet him. And, men, this is the same man who helps with dirty dishes, laundry, and a host of other household responsibilities. Small kindnesses and enthusiasm travels into the bedroom.

Always "prime the pump" with tender kisses, affectionate caresses, affirming words, hand holding, and love messages. Leave love notes in unexpected places. You can get pretty creative with lipstick. Look for ways you can express your love and never let the sparks fizzle.

You've found your *one-and-only*, your *endless love*, your *heart's desire*—this person you've chosen for life was created by God in His image. The way you love and respect your beloved can be an act of worship—even the very act of sex.

A person's godly character can be revealed in witnessing how he or she treats his or her spouse. When you honor your spouse, you honor God.

Love each other all out. "Drink and imbibe deeply, O lovers" (Song of Solomon 5:1).

# Discussion Questions

- Would you be willing to get professional help if your sex life needs help?

- What gives you the ability to trust someone? Talk through what you expect from each other in order to be able to trust.

- Talk about how a man is affected by what he sees. Share your thoughts on this. Ladies, refrain from any judgment; keep in mind God created him this way.

- What needs to happen for you to feel connected as a couple?

- What are daily ways you can convey your love for each other?

- Do you expect romance in your relationship? What do you define as romance?

- "What happens in the bedroom *stays* in the bedroom." Do you agree with this statement?

# Chapter Eleven
## Date Nights and Having Fun Together

I remember I was jealous. My husband and I were at a couple's church event when I noticed them. I can't remember their names or what they looked like, but I remember burning with intense jealousy, unable to focus on anything else.

Let's call them Jack and Sally for the sake of the narrative.

Jack arrived to the event first, without Sally. (I found out later that Sally had fallen behind, so they took separate cars to the event.) Hmm, quite unusual; most couples would stay home together and fight it out. When she arrived she was smiling, and he was smiling. Again, a bit unusual; one would expect *some* tension. They embraced. Glancing over—okay, staring—I looked for signs of discontentment, but I couldn't find any. I mean, Jack had gone ahead without her! Most would be at least a bit perturbed with the other. Nothing. No disgruntled signs at all. Hmm. As she sat down, Jack made a fun-hearted joke about her being late, saying, "She's on Sally Standard Time."

Everyone laughed.

Then Jack and Sally gave each other a high five!

This struck me in a powerful way. You need to understand that at the time Mike and I were immersed in raising small children. So much of our energy and communication was absorbed in what we deemed *serious issues*. As I watched this couple giving each other a high five—*at that very moment*—I became grossly aware of the fact that our marriage was lacking fun.

Noticeably, Jack and Sally had fun together. I longed for fun in my marriage. I coveted high fives.

When the time was right, I talked with Mike about my observation and evaluation of Jack and Sally, along with my own desire for shared fun.

"I want us to laugh and have fun. I want to give each other high fives." I put it out there, not sure how Mike would react.

He agreed! I was relieved but more so enormously excited. This was a momentous turn, bringing new life and vigor into our relationship. Since then, we've been strategic about having fun together. . .*including many high fives*. You would think it would happen effortlessly, and I suppose sometimes it does, but what if you turn into—like we did—one of those couples who don't naturally have fun together? Or maybe when life gets busy you put fun aside for *more important matters*. Many times, fun requires scheduling and planning.

We find time for what's most important to us, and scheduling regular date nights will give your marriage a boost. Make this a priority. Once a week, once a month, or once every two months—get date nights on your calendar. It can be going out for dinner, attending the theater, booking a hotel room for the evening, or as simple as taking a long walk with a stop under a tree—whatever fun activity you enjoy as a couple. Spend time together with just the two of you, the more often, the better. My recommendation would be once a week. When Mike and I were tight on funds, we'd grab a cup of coffee at a coffee shop and talk for hours.

What are the most fun dates? If you were to ask around, you'd find one common denominator: couples would tell you what makes their dates memorable and special is not so much the activity itself but the *time spent together*.

I know planning dates, for some men, can be very intimidating. Too often in marriage the best dates he planned were the ones you had while you were dating. Gentlemen, don't let this be the case. Continue planning dates after you're married, just like you did when you were dating. Don't reach your romance peak during your courtship. In other words, keep up the dates. Plan good ones. Ask her out. Woo her. I don't know what it is exactly, but we women love when our men have a plan—and then go for it. It just gives us a charge. Inside we're saying, "Oh yeah, that's my man!" Even if the date is lame, we'll still like it, as long as you execute it well.

This is how it works: You ask her for a date. You tell her what time to be ready. Give her guidelines on what to wear. Then execute. It can be as simple as taking her for a hot dog or going for a bike ride, but do it with confidence. As long as you seem sure of yourself, she'll go along. Going for a walk and stopping for ice cream? Do it with charm and be debonair. With each step, walk with certainty, and most importantly, give her your undivided attention. She'll be bragging about you so much you'll hear comments from other men like, "Dude, quit making us look bad!"

If she ever complains about any of your dates (which this

would be very foolish on her part!), then calmly say, "Next time you get to plan the date." Let her plan one if she wants to, but don't stop planning dates yourself.

Ladies—hello again—if after you're married and your husband plans a date for you, just say "Thank you" and enjoy it. Very few husbands do this. If yours turns into one of the very few, *thank the good Lord and sing a praise song, and never complain about a date!* When your husband thinks he cannot meet your expectations and fears letting you down, he'll be hesitant in making future dates and may even stop all together. Be wise; don't do anything to dampen his efforts.

It can also be fun to plan dates together.

Equally, ladies, by all means, you plan some dates, too— *without complaining.* I've planned many fun dates over the years. One time he arrived home to a note that said "Meet me at such-and-such restaurant." It was signed with a lipstick kiss. I also planned numerous dates at home, where I made a special candlelight dinner for two and got excessively dressed up. One family favorite over the years—after the kids arrived—was fondly referred to as Hot Dog Night. I'd make hot dogs for the kids (a treat they rarely got), with some finger foods, juice, and dessert, let them watch a movie, and put them to bed *early.* This cleared the night for *adult* fun. When I announced, "It's *Hot Dog Night!*" everyone was happy. It was an inexpensive way to have a fun date that didn't require a babysitter.

My husband and I have always had regular dates throughout our marriage. For years, once the kids got a little older, we've had a standing all-day date, once a week, on his day off.

After getting in the routine of our all-day dates, our "formal" dates slacked off a bit. Then, one day—after over thirty years of marriage—I sat across from him at a coffee shop while he was engrossed on his phone. And what was he doing? Yeah, I was wondering the same thing, too. It was taking *forever*. Sipping my coffee, I waited. By the time I was completely put out and feeling a bit neglected, he put his phone down, looked at me, and said, "There, I'm done."

"Okay," I responded, "done with what?"

"I've just put non-negotiable date nights on my calendar for the whole year."

Well, la-de-DA-DA! No longer was I put out. He took me from neglect to feeling like the awkward schoolgirl who just got asked out for the first time, and I think there may have been drool involved, too. At this point, I would have eaten ice pops in a snowstorm with him!

Here's the grand message about dating: schedule time together—no matter what—even through the baby years or graduate school, to career building, through caring for aging parents and retirement.

Never. Stop. Dating.

## Couples Who Play Together Stay Together

Have fun, celebrate, laugh, and live it up, because you can't have too much fun together. Having fun will not only propel you to the seventy-year yard line; it will make your relationship rock solid.

As a couple, there are many ways to have fun, and we are

going to explore some of those ways.

Our first stop: the bedroom.

*You sure write about sex a lot.* Yes, I do. And I will tell you why. Sex, to a vast degree, characterizes your relationship. It's what makes your marriage uniquely special over every other relationship you have. You can only have sex with your spouse. You can have coffee with a friend and talk and dream. You can play racquetball with your buddy. You can go on a vacation with a family member. But you can only have sex with your husband/wife, making sex a huge distinguisher.

What's number one on the list for fun?

Number one: exhilarating-electrifying-intoxicating...sex.

(You most likely need to take my word for it, *unless you're already married!*)

Number two: everything else.

Now, I'm aware some would disagree, but overall, most would agree with me. Sexual intimacy is one of God's greatest designs for marriage, and He wants us to have fun with His creation.

Hints on having the most fun in the love zone:

Men: Remember outward and then inward. Work on the outer extremities of her body before you tackle *the good stuff.* This includes affectionate touches throughout the day, as well as giving her a hand when she needs it with household chores and needs. It's true, few women can resist a man who does dishes and vacuums. Why do you think my husband makes our bed every day? Ahhh, now you're getting it.

Women: Dive right in. Abandon the girl he took home to meet Mama.

Consider how Dr. Kevin Leman puts it. He says a man feels a great sense of accomplishment when he can make his wife go wild in the bedroom and, as he puts it, "put a few scratches on his back in the heat of passion." Every man wants to know he can please his woman. Who he is as a man is extremely tied to how she responds to him sexually. He can still feel on top of the world even if he's struggling at work, has a body that is breaking down—or blowing up—if his wife finds him desirable and responds to him sexually.[1]

Ladies, this would be the biggest high five you could give him. He wants to please you inside and outside the bedroom. According to John Gray, PhD, *Venus on Fire Mars on Ice*, "The perfect partner for a man is a woman he can please" (80). Let's stop and pause right there. Take a few minutes to soak that in before you move on.

Showing displeasure with him in any way is very detrimental to a man's psyche. The way he does the dishes. How he folds the laundry. The restaurant he picked for dinner. The scenic route he took to the movies. Criticizing will eat away at your man and, consequently, your relationship. And, men, the same warning applies to you as well. Constant critiquing of her cooking (if she's the one doing the cooking) or whatever else will give her cause to doubt herself and erode trust.

## Celebrate

Always look for reasons to celebrate. Celebrate wins together. If one of you gets a promotion, have a party, even if it's just the two of you. If a goal is accomplished, rejoice together.

---

1 Leman, *Sheet Music*, 52.

Express joyful satisfaction for good decisions and earned rewards. When you can afford the new dishwasher, have a banquet. Notice what's good along the way of your everyday. Don't just gloss over all the wonderful gifts God brings— revel and celebrate each one, no matter how seemingly small.

Take interest in each other's hobbies. I've seen many couples allow hobbies to divide them. She'll go off for a weekend with the girls antique shopping, while he'll venture out with the guys for a golf tournament. Now, I'm not saying don't have friends whom you spend time with; on the contrary, enjoying time with friends is an important part of your overall emotional health. What I am saying is, make sure you don't neglect your time together, using up all of your extra time with friends at the expense of your relationship. Balance a trip with the girls with a trip with your man. Invite her to join you and take her on a date after your sports event.

Go on vacations together. Take the advice of my widowed neighbor. She told me she and her husband had always planned to take many fun trips and vacations together, but then he passed away. "Enjoy each other now," she said with resolve, "and do all the things you want to. Don't wait."

Many people have fallen into affairs because someone— other than their spouse—gave them attention. Make sure you are always the one giving your husband/wife the most attention. Don't allow anyone to out-give you in this area.

At the end of each workday, Mike and I spend some time together. Even when our kids were small they knew when Dad got home, Mom and Dad would spend time talking. We encourage, praise, listen, and cheer each other on. This is a habit we've maintained through the years. When you feel connected and unified, you can tackle just about any hindrance that could otherwise cause a barrier.

## Stay Connected

When we regularly show up for each other, we continue to learn about our spouse. Never stop learning about *WE*. What does he like to do in his spare time? What hobbies does she enjoy? Take interest in whatever your spouse takes interest in. Many times couples grow apart because they neglect to pay attention to each other. Even knowing the *little things* about your true love can connect you and reveal much about him/her. What's her favorite dessert? What does he take in his coffee? What games does she enjoy playing? Does he listen to the radio on the way to work? Putting *WE* before *ME* means persistently and intentionally learning about your spouse, not only focusing on your own interests.

Become a student of your spouse.

## The Cement Drug

There will be many choices and obstacles along the way of your life together; you set the pace on how you will react. I have found laughter joins you almost as much as sex. Almost.

Adam and Paige were engaged to be married and were visiting with Adam's extended family. His *whole* extended family—from grandparents to kids—gathered in the living room as Paige wrestled on the floor with one of the boys.

While playfully crawling on her hands and knees and hovering over one of the boys, somehow the buttons on her shirt unfastened—and, yes, her shirt flew open—exposing her bra and her 34Ds. *With Adam's family looking on!* Welcome to the family, Paige. Could you imagine? Most of us would have been mortified!

Adam and Paige laughed. When Paige told me the story, she was still laughing about it. She now, however, wears tank tops under her button-down shirts, but she's still laughing about it.

When awkward situations arise, look for the humor and laugh together. If Adam and Paige can laugh about giving his family a "show," you can laugh through less embarrassing life occurrences.

Laugh. High five. Move on. Can you think of a better alternative? Laughter really is a strong marital adhesive.

## Adventures

Try new things. When we try new things, we keep the relationship fresh. One idea would be to take up a sport together. If he participates in a sport, go with him. For many years Mike was on a men's softball team where I was the scorekeeper. We also played on a coed team. Currently, we work out together doing fitness programs at home. And on his bucket list, my husband has written, "*Ballroom dance classes together.*" Look for activities you can do as a couple.

One night while we were enjoying dinner with some close friends, Tony and Karen (their actual names, by the way), Tony talked about his many escapades as a softball umpire. I asked Karen if she had ever gone to watch him umpire. She hadn't. I suggested we all go. A few weeks later I got a phone call. "Lu, guess where I am? I'm at one of his games, and IT'S A RIOT! This is so fun. He's running everywhere! You've got to see this!" On the night that we all watched him umpire, my friend kept saying, "Look at my cute husband!" Never undervalue the power of showing up for each other.

Sometimes we need to create a little adventure. One leisurely Sunday afternoon, after we'd arrived home from church and after a long week of driving and taking care of our three kids, Mike told me he had a surprise planned.

He said, "Let's go."

"Wait, do I need to bring anything? When will we be back? What about the kids?"

"Don't worry about it. I took care of everything; just come with me."

So, I went along. Wouldn't you? We drove across town, and he dropped me off at a Starbucks, bought me a cup of coffee, handed me the book I was currently reading, and then. . .*he left*. This was a bit weird, but I enjoyed the reading time and I love coffee, so I was totally happy. Somewhere between finishing my coffee and becoming irritated that he was taking so long, Mike arrived back.

Again, he said, "Let's go."

"Where are we going?"

"You'll see."

And we drove. We pulled up to a hotel. *If this is about him "gettin' some," we could have done that at home. I'm really not that hard "to get." But, okay, it's still sweet. I'll go along.*

We got out of the car and walked to one of the rooms.

"Wait here," he said as he went into the room. "I'll just be a few minutes."

And I waited. He came back out and walked me into a dark hotel room. *All right, this is really getting weird now. Is there a whistle I can blow?*

Get ready, ladies and gentlemen, because it gets even weirder.

Then, he says, "Give me your clothes." *Say what? Are you kidding me right now? Geez! This is a little pushy, but I'll play along because he's sure gone through a lot of trouble for this.*

Then. . .he leaves!

I'm standing there in the dark. . .in my birthday suit! *Wait, he said something before he left. Something about the bathroom and instructions.* As my eyes adjusted to the dark, I reached over and open the bathroom door. Glowing light appeared. The bathroom was filled with candles, and a bubble bath had been drawn. Tears fell from my eyes. I could hardly read the letter he had left for me as the tears rolled down my face. Sweet words filled the page, along with instructions and the time he would be picking me up for our date. Not only was there a bath to enjoy, everything I needed was there, along with a dress and shoes for the evening. And the rest of the story is private, but I will say, it wasn't weird at all. This story stands as a reminder of how I can always trust him. Ladies, what woman wouldn't go to the end of the earth for a man like this? And, men, do you see why I'm excited to see his car pull up at the end of the day?

Keep it fresh; always create new adventure.

You may be thinking, *What constitutes an adventure?* An adventure is creating new experiences you can enjoy together. You have a clean slate to create adventure in your marriage. It doesn't have to be complicated or elaborate.

Let me give you real-life examples of ways married couples are creating adventure together:

Participating in chili cook-offs. Yes! I know a couple who regularly enter and judge chili cook-offs. They have often traveled to do so and have even been on TV.

Trying new restaurants. This couple actively seeks out new restaurants to try together. It's a hobby for them.

Hunting with a metal detector. Different, I know, but this couple purchased a metal detector and now they comb beaches looking for "finds." They enjoy their time together, and that's all that matters.

Browsing furniture stores. I knew of a couple who enjoyed walking through furniture stores. When they traveled, they would look for stores to visit.

Camping. Many couples enjoy creating adventure together by camping.

Attending concerts. Some friends of ours attend as many concerts as possible; they love it and it's a way they bond.

Playing BINGO. My parents play BINGO together— every night! They love it. I will often get early-morning calls about how much money they won the night before.

Finally, one of the best and most powerful—as well as most rewarding— adventures you can do is serving in ministry together. This will bond you, not only connecting you as a couple but connecting you closer to God as well. "Therefore, since we receive a kingdom which cannot be shaken, let us show gratitude, by which we may offer to God an acceptable service with reverence and awe" (Hebrews 12:28).

Hiking, gardening, fishing, boating, bowling, tennis, reading clubs, marathon running. . .find something you can enjoy and do as a couple.

Think of every day as an adventure, as you pen the pages of your marriage story—together, as *WE*. And give each other many high fives along the way. This is your story. This is your adventure. Together.

# Discussion Questions

- How will you create fun adventures together? Make a list of all the fun activities you want to do as a couple.

- Is there a ministry you can serve in together? Discuss options.

- How often would you like to schedule date nights? Consider putting dates on the calendar.

- What is the most fun date you've had? What did you enjoy most about it?

- Do you agree that "Couples who play together stay together"?

# Chapter Twelve
## Money, Money, Money

As a little girl I painfully watched my dad pull out a big shoe box overstuffed with envelopes and papers. He'd shuffle papers around, moan and groan. . .moan. . .groan. . .moan. . . groan.

"Daddy, what are you doing?"

"I'm going through all of our bills to see which ones I can hold off on paying."

Each time the shoe box made an appearance from the closet and onto the kitchen table, fear and anxiety poured into my little heart. I learned at a very young age that not having enough money to pay your bills was toxic.

Growing up with very little, my dad placed a high value on money and hated parting with it. It wasn't uncommon to hear him get into arguments with clerks, salespeople, and cashiers. He did whatever he had to do in order to pay as little as he possibly could. Unlike most men, my dad kept his cash in a money clip, not a wallet. It was almost as if he were saying cash could not sit in a wallet with other trivial things; it needed a special place of its own. I'm certain I heard Darth Vader's "Imperial March" any time cash was retrieved from his money clip. Too young to understand money value, I felt a sense of relief whenever he got change back, thinking at least there was *some* money left over. The message I got was when you get money, clench it tight, and only part with it when you absolutely have to.

By the time I was old enough to babysit—*for fifty cents an hour!*—I kept a mason jar with a minimum of fifty dollars safely tucked away in my sock drawer. (You do the math on how many babysitting hours that was.) Sometimes when my parents didn't have any cash to go out, they would borrow money from my jar and then pay it back at a later time. I felt like a superhero as I watched my dad unscrew the jar and take what they needed. I always made sure there was enough money saved—*just in case* Mom and Dad needed it.

Even today, it would be hard for me to feel safe if there weren't savings tucked away. In general, it can be difficult for me to spend money, especially on myself. (And you men are shouting, *"Hooray, the perfect woman!"*) I prefer to save it and give it away. And while that sounds noble and good, my husband jokes that if I had full control over our finances, I'd cause us to go without water and electricity so I could double the payment on the mortgage. (He's probably right, but I'll never tell him!) It stops being noble if you're acting out of fear rather than relying on and trusting in God. As I relayed this story to our adult daughter, she added, "Dad once told me, 'If your mother had complete control of our finances, she'd pay off all the bills, but we'd be *homeless,*'" then she and I both broke into laughter at the truth and absurdity of the statement.

My husband tends to be more balanced when it comes

to finances—this makes us a strong team—which is why I can sign all checks over to him with confidence. (And the men say, *"And it keeps getting better and better!"* Note: I'm not suggesting this method for everyone. You've got to do what works best for you.) Even my paycheck gets directly deposited into our joint account. The last time my pay voucher showed up in my e-mail, just for fun I thought I'd look at it and see how much I made. Do you know I was unable to open it? The church puts a password on all payroll vouchers. Ha! This made me laugh as I thought about the chapter I'm presently writing. For some this would cause anxiety, but for me, it brings peace. I totally trust my husband. Completely. I know the first thing he'll do is tithe, as well as give an offering to God. I know he'll pay whatever expenses we have. I know he'll overpay on our home mortgage, and I know he'll save. I know this because we have a plan. We talk about our finances and our future goals, and we are united.

Patty's story:

"My accountant husband and I have had our financial woes. You would think being married to an accountant would shield us from financial disaster. Wrong!

"After we were married it wasn't long before James learned how unintelligent I was about money. He was in the process of getting his accounting degree and was extremely surprised when a letter arrived from the IRS. I owed A LOT of money in back taxes.

"You need to know I'm a rule follower and law-abiding citizen. I had no idea I owed back taxes. When my employer handed me a piece of paper with W-2 written at the top, I threw it away. I mean, who keeps every little paper, right? I threw everything away! Well, as you could imagine, James was extremely flustered when the IRS letter showed up in our mail. He couldn't believe I had thrown my W-2's in the trash. I was freaking out crying. His character really shined through that night, because he was very kind and understanding when he could have really let me have it. He wasn't mean, but he was very stern. I did, however, get a lesson/lecture that could have awarded me an honorary accounting degree.

"After we got things all cleared up with the IRS, it still took a long time before I could be trusted to handle the checkbook again. I would do things like add withdrawals in the checkbook forgetting that you're supposed to subtract them. Again, he was very gracious with me.

"As time went on, I learned that *he* wasn't that good with money either. (Now it was my turn to be gracious.) Being the man of the house, he wanted to provide for his growing family. When a need would arise, and there was no cash, we would charge things. Unfortunately, this led to credit card debt.

"We quickly realized our money personalities. I became the saver. He became the spender. I saved because I was too afraid to balance the checkbook. He spent because he was all too comfortable handling the money.

"Now, we are a mix of the two. We discuss every purchase and break up our finances into several different categories. We budget out the entire year, month, and week to week. (I guess his accounting degree has helped us!) We also never purchase anything over a certain dollar amount without talking about it. We're not perfect, but this has certainly

helped prevent further financial woes or credit card debt, and
I don't throw away important papers anymore."


## Do You Really Want to Fight over Money?

Empires have been destroyed over money.

Many marriages have exploded due to money issues.

When our children started driving, our insurance agent
told us it was 100 percent likely they'd have an accident
within one year of getting their licenses. I have no idea
where our agent got this number from, but it wasn't the
case with our kids. One had an accident after two years, another after about five years, and—*beating all the odds!*—one
out of three, not at all. I can confidently say, *There is a 99.9
percent chance you will have conflicts about money.* I'd like to
say 100 percent, but as you can see from the predictions of
our insurance agent, nothing is 100 percent. So I'll play it
safe and say 99.9 percent.

Some of the most heated—*and most frequent*—arguments
couples have are over finances. My goal with this chapter
is to help you avoid this and give you a guide to harmony
with money matters. Ready? Pull out your wallet—or money
clip—because here we go!

"He who loves money will not be satisfied with money,
nor he who loves abundance with its income" (Ecclesiastes
5:10). Loving, caring relationships are what will satisfy us.
Stemming first from our relationship with God, and then our
relationship with our spouse. The closer you get to your Creator—the God of the universe—the more your true purpose

and value will be realized. Don't buy into the lie that material things will satisfy you.

How much do you need to have until you can say, "I have all I need"? Proverbs 27:20 says, "Sheol [Jewish term for place of the dead] and Abaddon [an angel known as the Destroyer] are never satisfied, nor are the eyes of man ever satisfied." We want more. . .more. . .and more!

When do you finally have enough? I enjoy watching the TV show *Shark Tank* where rich entrepreneurs allow business owners to pitch an investment idea. It's very fun to watch, but it always intrigues me to see how each entrepreneur is always looking for the next investment deal. It seems having millions or even billions of dollars is still not enough. When does enough become enough? Does it ever? Can we ever get to a place where we can say, "Okay, I'm good. That's enough." If you got there, would you know?

Understand that a lack of contentment is a spiritual problem—*not a money problem*. Contemplate what it says in 1 Timothy 6:10–11, "For the love of money is a root of all sorts of evil, and some by longing for it have wandered away from the faith and pierced themselves with many griefs. But flee from these things, you man of God, and pursue righteousness, godliness, faith, love, perseverance and gentleness." Establishing what's priority for *WE* will help you avoid financial destruction *and* strengthen your marriage.

Please hear this: the most important principle you need to learn—if you only get this from this whole chapter, I'd call it a big win—*get unified and be in agreement about money*. Spend, save, give, toss, smell, swell, stock, wrap, dress, bury, cook, balloon, manage, or breed it—agree to it.

"Don't take your spouse someplace where he/she is uncomfortable," says Rick Kasel, pastor of Stewardship & Estate Planning, Shepherd Church. This is great advice not only with regard to finances but also with all aspects of marriage. I was surprised to hear him say this as it related to his household financial decisions. He explained that he has knowledge and expertise in investing but never does anything with their money his wife feels uncomfortable with. Did you catch that? *He's* the one with the know-how, and yet, he consults his wife on matters of finance. Why? Because he wants her to feel safe, secure, and respected. *Men, write that down! It applies to how much fun you'll have in the bedroom!* "If she doesn't trust you financially, it will put a damper on your intimacy"—that's what Pastor Rick tells the guys when he gets them alone.

## To Tithe or Not to Tithe

Recognize that every penny you earn comes from God. It is "He who is giving you power to make wealth" (Deuteronomy 8:18). Your attitude about money, how you handle money, and how you approach what God says about money will have colossal ramifications for the breath and life of your marriage. "Every spending decision is a spiritual decision," says Ron Blue, author of *Faith-Based Family Finances*. The Bible is filled with many references to money. Why do you think God talks about money so much? Clearly, what we do with our money matters to God.

If you'll allow the Bible to be your guide, not only will you have less marital friction; you'll have peace. In light of this, partner with God and give Him what He requires. "Honor the LORD from your wealth and from the first of all your produce" (Proverbs 3:9–10).

The Bible tells us to honor God *first* with our wealth, not *wait and see what's left at the end of the month.* Give to God *first.* Jesus talks about tithing in Matthew 23:23: "Woe to you, scribes and Pharisees, hypocrites! For you tithe [a tenth] mint and dill and cummin, and have neglected the weightier provisions of the law: justice and mercy and faithfulness; but these are the things you should have done without neglecting the others." In other words, Jesus is saying you need to be tithing.

In Malachi 3:8–10 it says:

> *"Will a man rob God? Yet you are robbing Me! But you say, 'How have we robbed You?' In tithes and offerings. You are cursed with a curse, for you are robbing Me, the whole nation of you! Bring the whole tithe into the storehouse, so that there may be food in My house, and test Me now in this," says the LORD of hosts, "if I will not open for you the windows of heaven and pour out for you a blessing until it overflows."*

Pastor and author Barry L. Cameron says "tithing is elementary," and emphatically states that it's a *"starting point* for all believers" in Jesus Christ. If the devil can get you to disobey God in the area of tithing, he can hoodwink you to disobey in other areas as well, and rob you of the many joys and blessings God has in store for your life.[1]

God owns it all! If you don't believe me, attend an estate sale and watch what happens to earthly possessions. Once you're gone—*news flash: everyone dies*—all your stuff won't be "owned" by you anymore. It all goes back to God. We only get to manage it while we are here. This includes every dollar that flies into your hand. (Even the dollars you wrestle and wrangle to get!) The Bible is very clear in this: "The earth is the LORD's, and all it contains, the world, and those who dwell in it" (Psalm 24:1).

Barry L. Cameron also tells a story about Sir John Templeton, one of the world's most respected investors and investment counselors. Sir John Templeton helped hundreds of thousands of people with their wealth over a span of fifty-two years before retiring. There was one question Templeton was frequently asked: "What's the best investment?" Jumping at the chance to answer, you may find what he said surprising—touting it as the "best investment" anyone could ever make—tithing, giving at least 10 percent of your income to your church. He added that in all of his many years as an investment counselor, tithing was the one investment that "never proved faulty." He had never come across a family who tithed for as long as ten years that didn't become "prosperous and happy."[2]

---

1 Barry L. Cameron, *The ABC's of Financial Success* (Lily Dale, NY: HeartSpring Publishing, 2001), 76.
2 Ibid., 111.

I've heard the question raised, "I want to tithe, but my spouse doesn't want to. What do I do?"

This indeed is a tough question. I would say again, *get unified and be in agreement.* The amount you give needs to be an agreed-upon amount. You need to put *WE* before *ME.* Give as much as you both feel comfortable with. If you want to give 10 percent as instructed in scripture, or even more, as an offering, and your spouse doesn't—pray and wait. Let God turn the tide with your spouse; He can "move" better than you. First, honor your husband/wife, and let God take care of the rest. God doesn't need your money, but He desires to use your influence and your testimony.

## Plan

Consider Proverbs 6:6–8: "Go to the ant, O sluggard, observe her ways and be wise, which, having no chief, officer or ruler, prepares her food in the summer and gathers her provision in the harvest."

We live in Southern California where it's known for "never" raining—there's even a famous song about it originally released by Albert Hammond in the '70s. Are you singing it in your head? Or am I dating myself? Okay, give yourself a little history lesson and google it. *It never rains in Southern California.* . .yet, one morning, Mike and I were working out in our gym/garage when water *from the rain* started seeping through from under the garage door, crowding in on my dry workout space. It reminded me of when during a storm our garage was flooded, leaving structural damage and destroying much of what we had stored. Which wasn't as fun as the time my son, who was four years old at the time, ran to me from the front of our house excited to proclaim, "Mom, it's raining IN THE HOUSE!"

We always like to assume the storms are not going to hit us, but they do. It always rains at some point, even in Southern California! You need to plan on mishaps—a blizzard, snowstorm, hurricane, or rainstorm will hit you at some point—whether through a loss of a job, an illness, an accident, or an actual disaster. Plan on it. Save for it. Keep a reserve ready—*just in case*! Save "three to six months of expenses" according to Dave Ramsey in *The Total Money Makeover*.[3] You never know when your refrigerator will go out or your roof will start leaking; it's always best if you plan for misfortunes, *and* less stressful.

Without a plan you'll be drifting aimlessly on an inflatable raft with a tiny hole. As the air drains out of your *life raft*, one day you'll realize your lack of planning is running you, and not the other way around. You'll feel out of control. Floating. Desperate. Grasping for cash and wondering why you never achieved your dreams of financial freedom and success.

As you craft your money story, consider what your goals are.

How many of the same objectives do you agree on? I know of a couple who disastrously sailed into titanic marital problems because she thrived on experiences and adventure, wanting to travel as many places as she could, while he felt

---

3 Dave Ramsey, *The Total Money Makeover* (Nashville, TN: Thomas Nelson, 2013), 139.

most content staying home. Massive collision. There are endless scenarios. He loves to "enjoy" money as soon as he gets it, while she wants to save. She loves fancy furniture, clothes, and cars; he'd rather live in a small log cabin and cultivate the land. He likes to give large amounts of money to charities, while she thinks all their money should go to their church. He wants to travel through Europe; she wants to buy a house.

This does not mean you give up on your bucket list. This means you have two people working on your bucket list. . .and *two* bucket lists.

One of my all-time favorite vacations was going to the Winchester Mystery House with my husband. (The Winchester Mystery House is a mansion in San Jose, California, once owned by the late Sarah Winchester, the heiress to the rifle fortune.) Mike had talked about going for all of our marriage. (Buying a house and then having children slowed down our bucket list adventures. After thirty years, we finally went.) It was more exhilarating for me than if it had been on my own bucket list. I was as giddy as a kid experiencing Disneyland for the first time. I may have been even more excited than he was!

Construct a plan in which you both are satisfied and fulfilled and where you both consider the needs and desires of the other. It's okay to not want the same things. It's not okay to demean the other if he/she wants something different than you. No two people—*breathing people*—will always agree. Our friend Scott (his actual name) has a saying: "If you're right and you're rude, you're wrong." Putting *WE* before *ME* means you open your thinking to new approaches to life and are flexible about getting what you want.

Come up with a financial plan you can both agree to.


## Goals

One very successful business owner told me his biggest financial mistake was not starting his retirement plan when he was young. "I could retire right now if I wanted to, had I planned for the future," he told me as he sighed. "If only someone had told me that when I was young."

What are your marriage goals? Do you want to live in the town you're currently living in, or will you be moving? If you move, will your expenses change? Do you want to buy a house, or would you prefer to rent? How many bedrooms do you desire? Are there any trips you'd like to take as a couple? Do you plan on making any big purchases this coming year? Do you need to buy furniture? Is there debt you need to pay off?

What are you willing to do to achieve your goals?

When I was a child, the park across the street from my house sold ice cream for ten to twenty-five cents each. My friend and I discovered the sandbox with the uneven bars had change in the sand. (Looking back on it now, perhaps when parkgoers would hang upside down on the bars, the change would fall out of their pockets. We didn't know this as kids; all we knew was that we found change buried in the sand.) Any time my friend and I wanted ice cream—which was often; what kid doesn't want ice cream?—not having any money, we'd dig through the sand looking for buried coins. We didn't stop digging until we had enough change to buy *two* ice creams—sometimes we'd dig for hours. Those ice creams tasted better than any ice cream I've ever eaten my whole life, probably because of how hard we worked to achieve our goal.

Decide together what you want and what you are willing to do to get there. What's most important? What do you want to spend your money on? Do you agree? Get on the same page; be united and in agreement. Define your goals and write them down.

Before we continue on, think about what the Bible says in Matthew 6:19–21: "'Do not store up for yourselves treasures on earth, where moth and rust destroy, and where thieves break in and steal. But store up for yourselves treasures in heaven, where neither moth nor rust destroys, and where thieves do not break in or steal; for where your treasure is, there your heart will be also.'"

## Let's Talk Debt

Don't believe the lie telling you to buy, buy, buy in order to be happy, happy, happy. Unless you pay cash, cash, cash, you will have debt, debt, debt, which will leave you stressed, stressed, stressed, and struggling, struggling, struggling. What will this do to your marriage? Seriously ponder: "The rich rules over the poor, and the borrower becomes the lender's slave" (Proverbs 22:7).

My friend Nancy, who handles the finances for her family, told me she and John had gotten into a sizable amount of debt during the beginning years of their marriage. Desiring to be a "good wife," she didn't want to deny John anything he wanted. "He worked so hard," Nancy told me. "I didn't want to tell him no." Finally, when the debt became overwhelming, Nancy mustered up the courage to tell John the reality about their financial situation. "I never wanted to disappoint him, but in the end, that's exactly what happened," Nancy recounted with despair. Once Nancy was honest with John— *and they were unified and in agreement*—they tackled their debt as a team. Today John and Nancy are debt free, except for the mortgage on their house.

Debt can be deadly to the health of your marriage. Every bank, department store, furniture store, hardware store, clothing store, and we-got-it-all store wants to give you a credit card. Why? Because if they can get you to use a credit card and make interest payments THEY MAKE MONEY and YOU LOSE MONEY. Also, did you know people tend to spend more money when using a credit card? Would you swim in a lake with alligators? Don't be fooled; debt can be very dangerous.

How do you avoid going into debt? You don't spend money you don't have. It's wise to pray before making large purchases. And always agree before any purchase is made.

What happens when she stands in the way of that boat you want? What happens when he puts up a barrier for your dream vacation to Hawaii? Let's play this out. Okay, you've got your boat and she hates it. Worse yet, it causes conflict. Then let's say it costs more than you thought and you get behind on your bills. Or, you finally get him to agree to the fantasy vacation, but it doesn't turn into the enchanted trip you had hoped. Moreover, he resents you when the credit card bills arrive. Consider what this will do to your marriage. Wait until you both agree! Even if you have the money to buy what you want. What's more important? A boat? A vacation? Or your marriage? Sometimes putting *WE* before *ME* means holding off on or revising what *ME* wants.

If you are already in debt, get on a plan together and decide to pay off your debt. Dave Ramsey, financial coach, bestselling author, and radio host, has many excellent books detailing how you can do this. Many have gotten out of debt like my friends Nancy and John, and so can you.

## Sometimes You Just Gotta Do What Makes Sense

At the end of the financial day, it's your money and you get to decide where it goes. Several years back, our church began a campaign to build a new sanctuary. Mike and I had been saving for a new car for him. He was driving the old family van. We both agreed we would take the money we had saved for the car and give it toward the new building campaign. We decided together, and we gave it together. It was one of the most joyous offerings I've ever made.

But then, the old van kept breaking down. We added up all of the repair costs over the previous year and realized a car payment would actually be cheaper! Even our mechanic told us to put the van to rest. We decided to purchase a car, even though we would be taking on payments. We then paid off the car as quickly as we could. The main point is, *we were united and in agreement.* Was taking on a car payment a good financial decision? Probably not. We both prayed about it and wanted the money to be used for God's work. Was it a harder road for us? Yes, of course it was. If you want to call it a mistake, it was one we made unanimously, and therefore our marriage remained harmonious.

## How about You?

How do you become *united and in agreement* about money? You need a strategy. Set up a time and a place to meet. Imagine with me the process of serving a delicious gourmet meal. You start with an empty table and slowly bring out all the goodies! Beef Wellington, creamy scalloped potatoes, fresh greens lightly tossed in a lemon-olive-oil dressing, off to the side a chocolate soufflé for the grand finale. . .okay, yeah, this isn't going to be as fun as a gourmet meal, but it can be painless if you begin with the right attitude. You may even have some fun in the process. Maybe.

Approach your "business" meeting with other-centeredness. Bring no expectations to the discussion table, erase the money whiteboard, and begin by bringing honesty, integrity, and understanding to the table. As in all aspects of your marriage, consider the other person and what's best for *WE*. You are starting over as a couple—as a team—and you are clearing the slate.

Be honest about where you both are financially *before* you get married. Disclose all debts, whether you consider the debt major or trivial. One surefire way to destroy trust is to withhold information about debts only to have your husband/wife find out *after* you're married.

You both came from different financial backgrounds. Just because your parents did things a certain way doesn't necessarily mean that way is best for you.

Sit down together and go over all of your financial responsibilities. Do you have a car payment? How much is your combined income? What will your expenses be? Agree on where you want your money to go and how you will spend your excess income. Are you stopping for coffee in the morning? How about an afternoon pastry? Have you ever added up how much "little stops" cost each month? Is this where you really want your money to go? Take a realistic look at where you are spending your money.

Then decide what you value most and where you want to invest your resources and energies. This is not a matter of right versus wrong. Traveling may be more important to you than buying a house. Living near family, or having the resources to visit family, may be a top priority for you. Maybe you don't mind cutting back in other areas so you can go to the movies or eat out twice a week. Maybe buying a house is on the top of your list and you're willing to go without certain luxuries to save.

Talk through all of your desires and, more importantly, how you can both have peace and security within those wants.

Here's a beginning easy-to-do harmonious-marriage-money strategy:

- Get on a budget

- Make all bank accounts joint accounts
- Agree before you spend a certain dollar amount
- Agree to tithe a minimum of 10 percent to your church
- Be in agreement about which one of you will manage your finances or if it will be both of you
- Have regular "business" meetings to discuss your finances
- Agree to live within your means; in other words, don't spend money you don't have
- Agree to save a certain amount every month
- Avoid debt and/or pay off any existing debt as soon as possible

The main objective is to get on the same team, map out a money strategy, and learn how you can work together making *WE* stronger.

# Discussion Questions

- Do you think it's important to tithe? Why or why not?

- Did your parents tithe?

- How was money handled in your home? Who managed the family finances, your mom or your dad?

- Did you feel secure financially as a child? Was there any fear involved about your family's security?

- Did you usually get what you wanted as a child?

- Will you have a joint bank account? Or do you plan on keeping separate accounts? If so, why?

- How important is saving money for you?

- Discuss the importance of being *united and in agreement* about money matters.

# Chapter Thirteen
## Marriage Is Forever; Don't Say the *D* Word

We were broken. Two broken people came together. This was our reality when Mike and I found each other. For decades we've worked at loving, forgiving, and mending two broken souls. This was especially true before we both became Christians—then we learned to offer all of our brokenness to God. Our heavenly Father continues to mend us a little more each day.

It's God's job to mend us; it's our job to do the work. Throughout this book we've unpacked tools, gotten into the nitty-gritty of marriage, and looked at some honest truths. I applaud you for getting to the last chapter. We're almost done. . .keep reading. Before we move on, and before you move into marital merriment, I'd like to ask you one critical question: Are you willing to do the work—the *hard* work of loving, forgiving, and sacrificing for another broken person?

Not all of us know how to do this, which is why preparing for marriage by reading this book and discussing the hard questions will set a solid foundation for you. As a new bride, I know I didn't have the tools I needed. Even worse, I entered marriage with the worst possible mind-set. As a young nineteen-year-old, it was all about *ME*. In fact, roughly two weeks before my wedding day I announced to my dad, "If it doesn't work out, I'll just get a divorce." Yes, I said it. I said the *D* word! Oh, and did I mention *my dad was paying for the wedding?* Not exactly what a father wants to hear.

Jumping into marriage naive and selfish, mixed with a whole lot of stupid, was a recipe for disaster and a prescription for pain. Somewhere along the way, God got a hold of me. I learned the key to fulfillment and contentment in marriage was shifting from *ME* to *WE.* There is no room for selfishness in marriage. *WE* needs to come before *ME,* and be considered in all things. That's when your marriage becomes supernatural, and even. . .well. . .*mystical.*

Sometime after the white dress comes off and returning from your honeymoon. . .reality will hit. Instead of all your problems being fixed, you'll have a double set of problems. Listen to the great news though: you'll also have a double set of hands, ears, brains, and hearts as long as you work together as a team—one united front—putting the other above yourself. Be committed to this. Fight for it.

## When WE Becomes Three. . .or More

Do you plan on having children? Sadly, some decide to expand their family thinking, *A baby will fix all of our problems.* This could not be further from the truth. There is no exchange for doing the work a solid marriage requires. Once you add children to your story, this adds an entirely new dynamic to your relationship. The health of your marriage will never be more critical than when you become a parent. What will your legacy be? Never deceive yourself or underestimate the power, whether good or bad, your marriage will have on your children. And please don't ever diminish the long-range destruction divorce would have on your entire family, especially your kids.

During a ministry group meeting, a handful of us were preparing for an upcoming children's event. Mentioning the chapter I was currently working on, Dane said, "My parents got divorced when I was three." All eyes were on Dane as we listened to his story. "I know I was young, but I remember the day my dad left. My parents were upstairs arguing. I remember my dad walking down the stairs with his luggage and then leaving." A tear rolled down his cheek. "I asked, 'What's going on? Where'd my daddy go?' The answer I got was, 'He left. We're getting a divorce.'

"This left my mom to take care of four kids alone. The pressure was way too much for her, and my dad didn't help much. I remember Mom and all of us kids waiting for a check to show up in the mailbox so we could eat. Sometimes the check never came, and we missed meals. I remember waiting on the front porch for my dad to pick me up and him never showing up." Multiple tears now flowing from his eyes, he said, "From the time I was a child I vowed I would always take care of my kids. After my divorce that's what I did. I raised all three of my kids on my own, and now I'm helping with my grandkids."

Dane is fifty-five years old and his parents' divorce still impacts him today. I've heard countless stories, from young children to teenagers and adults, of the devastation divorce caused in their lives. I'm sure you've heard them, too. You may have experienced it yourself.

Please hear this: one of the best gifts you can give your children is a home where Mom and Dad love each other and have a strong marriage.

## Rough Waters

A pastor once told me he gets calls on a regular basis from people unhappy in their marriages. "After listening to the caller complain about their spouse, I'll often get requests to call their husband/wife," he said with frustration. "But I always tell the person on the phone to have their spouse call me. They want a quick fix for their marriage, a painless fix of some magic call from a pastor who will 'straighten out their husband or wife,' but there is no such thing. They need to do the work marriage requires, and usually they have become lazy. They don't want to put in the work. They think one call from me can fix their spouse, when in reality *they* are probably the problem. At the very least, they are half of the problem."

What will you do when "happy-ever-after" turns into "battle-of-the-sexes"? (And, yes, I know, I know, it's "happ*ily* ever after." I just like "happy" better.) Many couples have their first big fight and don't have the tools to solve it without casualties—usually in the form of hurt feelings and nasty words they wish they could take back. After a fight it's like marital triage; you need to sort out which wounds need "medical attention." Wars leave wounded people who need fixing. Give each other the time, effort, and attention needed to feel secure in your marriage again.

Nicole shared one such story with me:

"My husband and I were newly married and both working full-time jobs. Arriving home at the end of our workdays, we'd first change into our comfy clothes, and then I would head to the kitchen while he headed to the TV. Dinner was like a workout for me. I wasn't a good cook—like his mother was—and the pressure to make a meal worthy enough to compare to his mom's heightened my anxiety. After dinner I would clean the kitchen—which took up the rest of my evening—while my "prince charming" would channel surf.

"This pattern went on for several months until one night I totally erupted. Feeling justified and oppressed, I stomped into the living room and interrupted his TV time. Once I got his attention, I launched a wet, dirty dish towel...hitting him square in the face. This was my call to justice! Our first BIG fight ensued, with tempers blazing, both trying to out-yell the other.

"After a long battle we finally calmed down and talked rationally. We came to an agreement that after work we would both prepare and clean up dinner. His kitchen skills were not any better than mine, but we enjoyed our time together.

"We quickly realized doing things the way 'your parents did' doesn't always work for you. I was trying to be an amazing cook and wife—like his mom—and he was merely modeling what his dad had done. We learned this lesson the hard way, but it was a valuable lesson to learn."

## What's Your Mindset?

This couple knew the only choice they had was to work things out.

" 'For I hate divorce,' says the LORD" (Malachi 2:16). And in Matthew 19:6, Jesus says, "So they are no longer two, but one flesh. What therefore God has joined together, let no man separate." Enter marriage with the mindset that there is only one option when rough waters roll in, and that is to work it out.

Yet, I know there are some of you reading this who have been divorced and are getting married again. You may have not had a choice. Your spouse left and—*no matter how much you pleaded or suggested getting help*—you couldn't change his/her mind. This happened to my friend Liz. Her husband asked her out to dinner and a movie. During dinner he announced, "I'm not happy. I'm moving out." Then, *he took her to a movie!* Liz was in shock! No matter what she tried, he refused to work things out. In the end, he divorced her.

Don't dismay, just because you've got a divorce in your past it doesn't mean you will have a repeat of your previous marriage. Learn as much as you can from your experience, and then focus on your current engagement/marriage and working at being the best husband/wife you can. You can still have your happy-ever-after. Believe it! Don't allow fear or what happened before to poison your current relationship. In other words, don't bring your ex-spouse with you into your new marriage. Start fresh, and don't hold on to regret or bitterness. Offer forgiveness to yourself and your ex-spouse.

Many of the strongest, happiest, and most fulfilled

marriages are those in which one or both spouses have been married before. Instead of focusing on what their ex-spouse did wrong, they focus on what they can do *now* to be the best husband/wife, using past experiences to learn and grow in their current marriage. Many times when we are given a second chance we cherish it more; this has certainly been my observation with many of these happy couples. When a divorce is in one's past, it's extremely unusual to find that person in a thriving marriage, if he/she hasn't accepted at least part of the responsibility for the previous breakup.

Right now. This minute. Determine divorce will not be part of your story. Commit to doing the essential work in order to secure a happy, thriving marriage. Can you agree to do this? Very well, let's cruise on to a non-negotiable blueprint and establish patterns for healthy communication and how to expose potential relationship killers.

## Squabbles

The majority of your battles—fights, passionate discussions—will stem from miscommunication and/or a lack of communication.

At times, it can be hard to imagine how you will *get through it* when you're in the middle of a big fight. New brides have called me in tears, fearful, "It's over." Her new groom stormed off, and she's sobbing and feeling hopeless. When a fight ensues, your feelings may be so intense that you feel stuck and unable to untie yourself. If this ever happens—and I truly hope it doesn't, and it most certainly won't if you take heed to the guidelines in this chapter—take a deep breath, seek God, and trust your vows. You will get through it. Strive to resolve the conflict; then your tomorrows will look much brighter, and your marriage will grow stronger.

One newly married couple got into their first huge passionate discussion and didn't know how to handle it. Do you know what they did? They wisely contacted the pastor who did their wedding ceremony and asked for help to resolve their disagreement. Their first stop after their big fight broke out was the church. There they received the communication tools needed as well as instruction on how to handle disputes better in the future.

Selfishness—wanting what *ME* wants—is the foundation of most arguments. Take a moment to consider James 4:1–2: "What is the source of quarrels and conflicts among you? Is not the source your pleasures that wage war in your members? You lust and do not have; so you commit murder. You are envious and cannot obtain; so you fight and quarrel." Any time a disagreement ensues, ask yourself the question *How am I being self-centered in this situation?*

At some point you will experience disharmony. How you handle conflict will determine how strong your marriage will be. You can choose to allow challenges to grow you and to mold you to be more Christlike. One way to achieve this is to talk about how you will handle disagreements, *ahead of time.* What will you do to resolve conflict?

Establish marriage ground rules:

- Commit to working all conflicts through

- Acknowledge you will work it out in the end
- Be secure in knowing you will forgive each other
- Agree to get help when you can't resolve issues on your own
- Commit to pray about challenges
- Agree to use the Bible as your guide

Know with certainty when disagreements break out that there is one—and only one—option, and that is to work it out, along with the reassurance you will forgive each other. No matter what nasty words were spoken. No matter how much you've been hurt or have hurt the other. You will forgive. You will work it out. There is no turning back—you have the other's back. It was many years into my marriage before I felt this kind of assurance. Once I did, it changed everything about my marriage. Give each other the gift of starting out with this security, and promise that you will always work things through.

Any time a problem or challenge arises in your marriage, always look at yourself first. Do a gut check. What's your part in the disagreement? In order to figure this out, you need to *listen*. Instead of constructing what your responses will be, listen when your mate talks. Too often, we are more concerned about what we are going to *say* rather than what we *hear*. We need to reverse this. Actively listen. And then take responsibility for your actions.

Do you have unrealistic expectations?

Consider how Kyle Idleman expands on this point in his book *The End of Me*.

*We are bombarded with movies and songs with one central theme in their message, the right partner will fill all of our needs and longings. "You complete me" is a common thread heard throughout movies and songs, and one many tend to subscribe to, expecting this unattainable goal from their spouse. We get married with massively false expectations leaning to another to fulfill us, placing an unrealistic burden on them. One of the most joyous and delightful gifts God has given us is romantic love—few things in life can compare with love's jubilation—but only our relationship with Jesus Christ can fulfill us completely and permanently.[1]*

I can't tell you the number of times Mike and I would have a dispute and solving it was a prayer or a Bible verse away. For real! Any time I feel utter despair, I open my Bible and/or ask God for guidance. Sometimes I need to apologize. Sometimes I need to understand the situation from my husband's view. Sometimes I need to express my deep hurt in order to gain greater intimacy and acceptance. It takes courage to do any of those options. It takes courage to admit when you're wrong and ask for forgiveness. It takes courage to risk your own feelings to understand another's. It takes courage to expose weaknesses, messiness, and brokenness. If there is ever a time to be brave, it's with your spouse—and sharing your *messiness*.

As we talked about in chapter three, when you understand the source of all hope, love, and forgiveness, then you can extend that same hope, love, and forgiveness to your

---

1 Kyle Idleman, *The End of Me* (Colorado Springs, CO: David C. Cook, 2015), 126–27.

beloved. Give heed to what the Bible says: "If someone says, 'I love God,' and hates his brother, he is a liar; for the one who does not love his brother whom he has seen, cannot love God whom he has not seen" (1 John 4:20).

Who is the closest "brother" to us? Our spouse. If you love God, you will love your spouse. Remember, in marriage *love* is an action word. How would you act if you were trying to convince him/her to marry you? Act that way every day. If only one of you does this, you'll have an amazing marriage. If both of you do this, you'll have a mind-blowing, mystical marriage, one that will feel like a fantasy. God created marriage, and when you do marriage the way God says, you get a marriage that's God-sized.

Oftentimes the secret sauce to accomplishing this type of marriage is in taking care of you. What? I know this sounds contrary to everything stated previously—you'll have to follow me through on this. If you are not in balance, it throws off the team. *You* need to keep *you* healthy—mentally, spiritually, and physically—in order to have balance in your relationship.

As soon as you stop working on being the best version of you, it will hurt *WE*. I know of a new bride who quit her stressful job because it interfered with being the best wife she could be. I know of a new groom who shifted his hours at work to spend more time at home with his wife. Do whatever you need to do in order to maintain balance.

Mentally: Keep your mind active. Seek out friends who inspire you and whom you can inspire. Always keep learning and growing as a person.

Spiritually: Be intentional about growing in your

relationship with God. In order to grow, this requires time and learning. Be in church every week. Spend time with God daily. And be active in serving in a ministry. The best way to find the best ministry for you is to stop and think about what excites you and what you have passion for. This is a huge clue into the perfect ministry for you. Don't think about it too long—jump in and serve.

Physically: Stay fit. It's unfair to you and to your spouse for you to "let yourself go." Find some form of exercise, and do it on a regular basis. Walk. Take the stairs. Find a workout program you can do at home. Join a gym. Do *something* to stay fit.

Eating healthy and taking time to rest is just as important for overall physical fitness. We need to rest and recuperate. What do you fuel your body with? Fueling your body with junk will leave you feeling like junk. If you are being destructive to your body, it can create a barrier to giving *your body* to another person. Get my drift?

When you neglect *ME*, you neglect *WE*. When you hurt *ME*, you hurt *WE*.

## Cultivate Your Marriage

### Church

If there was one thing you could do to massively improve the health of your marriage, would you do it? Would you?

Check this out: "Simply stated, couples who go to church or other religious services together on a regular basis have the lowest divorce rate of any group studied, regardless of other factors such as how long they've been married," says Shaunti Feldhahn in *The Good News about Marriage*.[2] And, "New tabulations of the Barna data that include church attendance, as well as the findings of several other studies, show that when a person attends church, it lowers their chances of divorce by roughly 25 to 50 percent compared to those who do not attend."[3]

I'd say that's a pretty good reason to go to church with your spouse each week. Wouldn't you?

"The pastor said if you want a strong marriage," Stacy emphatically stated, "sit in the front row in church service every week." You'll find Stacy and John in the front row every week, and it's no surprise that they do, indeed, have a strong marriage.

### Sex

Keep your marriage running on high-octane with a fulfilled, unselfish, mutually satisfying sex life.

Give serious consideration when Dr. Kevin Leman says that sex is a basic need for a man. A man who is fulfilled in this area of his life will have enormous amounts of appreciation and will act on such gratitude. Patting himself on the back for marrying his wife, he will drive home thinking he's *the happiest man alive* and plan out ways to make her feel special. You want him to willingly stop by the store on his way home or take care of your honey-do list? Meet his needs

---

2 Shaunti Feldhahn, *The Good News about Marriage* (Colorado Springs, CO: Multnomah, 2014), 74.
3 Ibid., 85.

sexually, and he'll be eager to help you. A man who feels sexually satisfied will not be distant—and when you talk to him, he'll want to hear what you have to say![4]

What woman doesn't want a husband like that, and what man wouldn't agree with this? Cultivating and keeping your sex life a priority will pay off in huge dividends for your marriage. When you have long lapses of sexual intimacy, it's like putting a wedge between you. Your relationship can still be good, but it's not operating on high-octane. Think of a brick wall. Sex is the mortar between the bricks. It cements you together.

## Time

Be mindful of the amount of time you spend together as a couple. Many couples drift apart, not due to any huge marital infraction but because they stopped securing time for each other. Happy couples make time for each other. One of the biggest warning signs on the road to a failing marriage is a lack of time together. Repair the problem—don't get stuck in a huge pothole. If you're not spending time together, you are growing in different areas and cultivating your life separately. Any time you have large gaps of connection with your husband/wife, a humongous flashing alarm needs to go off in your head. Warning! Warning! Marriage malfunction!

When you feel separated, schedule *WE* time. Agree to stay connected and to place time together as a top priority. We've all heard, "I wasn't happy," from someone who left their spouse, and the oh-so-common, "We grew apart." How do you think

---

4 Leman, *Sheet Music*, 46.

this happens? It happens when couples fail to cultivate their relationship, and slowly eliminate time for each other.

After you have children, if you choose to do so, finding alone time can become a challenge. Throughout your marriage you will go through various seasons. Understand "the kid season" is just that—*a season.* Eventually they will leave, and you'll be staring at each other with either a renewed vigor for your future alone years together or shattered by the broken pieces of your marriage you need to repair.

One way couples create their own divide is by having their children sleep with them. A friend of mine asked one such couple, "I don't mean to be rude, but how do you have sex if you have a two-year-old in your bed?" The answer she got was, "We don't." Okay. What? Warning! Warning! Marriage malfunction! Keep your bedroom a sanctuary for you as husband and wife.

Invest your time wisely. No matter how busy you might get at work, with your kids, or volunteering your time for church work, be strategic to nurture your relationship. Make whatever adjustments necessary in order to keep your marriage refreshed.

Once a week I work with a group of teenage girls at our church. Every week I have a scheduled "coffee date" with my husband before youth group. Look for ways you can "meet up" when your calendar fills up. When you were dating, you always seemed to find ways to "connect." Don't stop after you're married.

Protect your marriage by preserving your time together—no matter what season you're in.

## Never Say the *D* Word

"Seems like every time we have a conflict he throws the *D* word around," Denise told me. "Well, maybe you should just leave me." Or "If you feel that way, then let's just get divorced!" Or "Maybe we'd be better divorced then?" No, no, no, no! Never toss the *D* word around. *Ever.* It will cause tremendous insecurity in your spouse and hurt him/her, you, and your marriage. Statements like these are off-limits! Make a pact that these types of statements will never be uttered. Don't even allow yourself to think such things in your head either. Instead think, "What can I do to improve myself in order to improve my marriage?"

## Got Grit?

Do you have grit? Grit is what it takes to achieve your happy-ever-after. We all want happy-ever-after, don't we? Do you want a fairy-tale marriage? You can have it. Do *you* believe it? By now I'm sure you've heard negative proclamations about marriage, and people trying to burst your happy-ever-after bubble. Don't listen to any of it!

Many have unhappy marriages because they stopped doing the work. Somewhere along the way they lost their grit. Have the fortitude to be undeterred. Be a pit bull when it comes to working at and fighting for your marriage. Pit bulls are known for finishing a fight. Many have been shot because they *just wouldn't let go.* You're at the starting line of "Till death do us part," so grab on like a pit bull—*and dodge all the shots!* Remember the words of Jesus, "So they are no longer two, but one flesh. What therefore God has joined together, let no man separate" (Matthew 19:6).

Are you ready for the most exhilarating ride of your life? Develop tenacity, determination, and resolve; hold on tight—*like a pit bull*—when it comes to nurturing your marriage. Decide you will do the work that a happy, thriving marriage requires each and every day. Never stop making your marriage better. Never. Let. Go.

Love and enjoy each other.

Thank God for her daily. Be understanding with her, and never stop telling her how beautiful she is to you. Treasure her always.

Thank God for him daily. Respect and cherish him. Let words of praise overflow every day.

I'm so thankful I've been able to be part of your marital journey. Please know I've prayed for you. May God's blessings overflow as you begin your story of *WE* and craft your fairy-tale marriage.

# Discussion Questions

- What needs to happen for both of you to feel assured that you will always work out all of your disagreements? Even if agreeing is defined by agreeing to disagree. Discuss your answers.

- Establish ground rules for disagreements.

- Discuss what you will do to ensure regular time together.

- Do you plan on having children? If so, discuss what your expectations are.

- Are you planning on attending church together? Do you think church attendance would enhance your marriage?

- What steps do you need to take in order to stay balanced as individuals and as a couple?

- Discuss what it means to do "the work" as it relates to marriage.

- What will you do when you can't seem to settle arguments on your own?

- Are you willing to reach out for help, either from an older, more experienced couple or a pastor or professional counselor?

# About the Author

Lucille Williams may be a pastor's wife now, serving in ministry with her husband at one of the largest churches in America, but as an engaged eighteen-year-old, she had no idea what a healthy marriage looked like. A year later, it didn't stop her from saying "I do." With few marital tools mixed with foolishness and bickering, it was a recipe for disaster.

After the first "glorious" years of their relationship, which she now tags as the Five-Year-Fight, both she and her husband became Christians. That was the turning point. It wasn't perfect. It wasn't pretty. But through prayer, seeking God, wise counsel, teamwork, and crazy amounts of tenacity, Lucille's marriage developed into a highlight reel of her best moments instead of a war zone leaving devastation and fallout. Today she would describe her marriage as vibrant, thriving, happy, and spicy.

Lucille has been working with couples and families for over twenty-five years. Her background of service has led her home church to commission her as an individual who has been called to ministry. While greatly involved in ministry with her husband—the children's pastor at Shepherd Church in Porter Ranch, California—she also speaks at retreats, classes, and conferences.

Lucille enjoys working in ministry alongside her husband, Mike, of thirty-four years, and has an intense passion for ministering to families and young people. As a champion of marriage, she is greatly involved with marriage ministry and conducts premarital and marital coaching. In addition, she loves being on staff at Shepherd Church as the Family Theatre Director. Her position requires developing a creative and engaging show, directing a large team in producing a weekly production allowing families to come together and laugh while learning about God.

But she will tell you her greatest achievement is her family. It may sound cliché, but her favorite activity is hanging out with her husband, children, and grandchildren. Sitting around a dinner table with her family filled with laughter, pasta, and cake stands as her most adored event.

Lucille zealously loves her husband, kids, grandkids, cocker spaniel, and peanut butter. You can find more resources from Lucille by visiting her blog at LuSays.com.